50p

KU-416-733

EVERYDAY FUN BOOK

Marshall Cavendish

Magic
Compiled by: *Peter Eldin*
Illustrated by: *Grahame Corbett*

Nature
Compiled by: *Chris Maynard*
Illustrated by: *Barbara Firth*

Craft
Compiled by: *Eve Barwell*
Illustrated by: *Chris Legee,*
Neil Lorimer, Janet Allen, Victoria Drew

Science
Compiled by: *Neil Thomson*
Illustrated by: *Tony Hannaford*

Games
Compiled by: *Richard Kennedy*
Illustrated by: *Phil Dobson*

Hobbies
Compiled by: *Pinkie Martin*
Illustrated by: *Janet Allen*

Puzzles
Compiled by: *Bruce Leigh*
Illustrated by: *Malcolm Livingstone*

Borders
Illustration by: *Niki Daly*

*With grateful thanks to the pupils
of Allfarthing Primary School,
Wandsworth; Cestria County Junior and
Infant School, Chester-le-Street; Clockhouse,
Bradford Grammar School and Dubmire
Junior School, Houghton-le-Spring,
who tested the projects*

Published by
Marshall Cavendish Books Limited
58 Old Compton Street
London W1V 5PA

© Marshall Cavendish Limited 1978 – 84

ISBN 0 86307 168 6
Printed and bound in Italy by New Interlitho SpA.

THIS VOLUME IS NOT TO BE SOLD IN AUSTRALIA,
NEW ZEALAND OR NORTH AMERICA.

About this book

This colourful book is packed with 365 exciting things to make and play. There's something for everybody between six and twelve years old – for rainy indoor days, outdoor days, or just those 'What-shall-I-do-next?' days.

You'll find seven different kinds of projects: magical performances, nature-watching, craft, scientific fun, games to play, hobbies to amuse you, and puzzles to work out. You can identify each one of them by the colour behind the number above each project. There's also a code guide:

easy   harder

not-so-easy   ask an adult

Dip in wherever you like or begin at the very beginning. Or you could work your way through all the easy projects first and go on to the harder ones if you use the Project Guide in the back of the book. Before you start, read about the projects on these two pages, and look through the 'Useful things to know' on the next two.

Magic

This section shows you how to do magic tricks. Some performances will need secret preparation; others can be set up right before someone's eyes. When you become a practised magician, you could put on a big magic show.

If you want to find a magic project, look for blue in the border as shown above. It will have the number of the project in it.

Nature

In this section you will learn to observe nature and to watch how things grow and change. There are also lots of ideas for making things with finds from the natural world.

Some are 'all-year-round' projects, and others are 'afternoon' ones.

Find all the nature projects by looking for the bright green colour behind the project number.

Craft

'Craft' means doing things by hand. This section shows you how to make things from many different materials in all kinds of clever ways. You can be artistic (or messy!) but you are sure to enjoy yourself, whatever happens!

Look for the colour pink with a number on it when you want to do a craft project.

Science

Learning about science is fascinating when you make things that prove scientific laws. The science section shows you how to do this.

Some of the projects will amaze your friends; some will amuse you for hours; others can be turned into games to play.

Purple behind a number indicates that the project is a science one.

Hobbies

Saving things and searching for others is what this section is all about. Of course, you can't save things in just a day, but you can make a special display of things you have been collecting. Keep a very special hobby going forever, if you like! You will know the hobbies section by the sea-green colour behind the project number.

Puzzles

Spend your quiet hours with this section. Some of the puzzles are picture ones; some are geometric; others are mathematical and a few are word puzzles. You can recognise the puzzle section by looking for the colour yellow with a number on it.

The answers to most of the puzzles are in the back of the book. Don't peek first!

Games

This section really needs no explanation! Everyone plays games – sometimes on their own, sometimes with one other player, sometimes with lots of people at a party. There are all kinds to play in the games section. A few will be old favourites, others will be new and different.

When you want to play a game, look for a light-brown colour above the project.

A SQUARE CAN BE DIVIDED INTO TWO TRIANGLES

THIS TRIANGLE COMES FROM A SQUARE

THIS TRIANGLE COMES FROM A RECTANGLE

THIS TRIANGLE HAS THREE EQUAL SIDES

FOUR OF THESE CAN BUILD A PYRAMID

Useful things to know

There are 365 projects in this book and many different materials are used. Here are a few: tin cans, matchboxes, bottles and jars, lolly or ice-cream sticks, paper-bags, nuts and bolts, corks, pebbles, shells, cotton reels, buttons. Some other important ones are explained on these two pages. So don't throw anything away! Save up old newspapers and magazines, too. Use spare ones to cover your work surface.

All the things you will need for a particular project appear in **bold letters like these.** Read through each project first, then get together all the things you will need. And remember to clear up after you have finished!

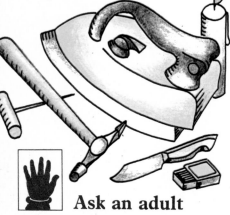

Ask an adult

When you see the sign of a hand in the border of a project, *always* ask an adult to help. The hand is a warning *never* to use the tools or materials listed here on your own:
Nails for punching holes and for building.
A **hammer** to bang in nails.
An awl to punch holes.

An iron for pressing leaves or cloth.
Spills (long tapers which burn when lit with a match) for a science experiment.
Candles, also lit with a match.
A penknife for cutting thick materials.
Glass for building projects.
Matches, if they need to be struck.
You will also see **'ask an adult'** to remind you not to take things which don't belong to you without asking permission first.

Drawing tools

You will find these materials in a stationer's or art shop.
Felt-tipped pens can be used on paper or cardboard instead of paints.
Wax crayons can also be used to colour paper and cardboard and can cover over other colours.
Waterproof Indian ink *must be used with great care* as it won't wash off if you spill it on anything.
Pair of compasses – is very useful whenever you need to draw a circle of a particular size.

Paper and cardboard

Most paper and cardboard can be bought at a stationer's or art shop.
Tracing paper is see-through.
Greaseproof and wax papers won't let sticky things cling to them. (They can also be used for tracing.)
Edible rice paper can be eaten!
Gummed paper shapes have paper backs which you peel off to get a sticky surface.
Cardboard comes in all colours and thicknesses. The project will tell you if you need a special kind (stiff or thin, for instance).
Glasspaper has a rough surface and is used for smoothing off cut edges of wood. Buy it from a hardware or do-it-yourself shop.

Paint and varnish

Wherever you see **paint** in a project you will also need a **paintbrush** (unless the project states otherwise).
Acrylic paint can be used on paper and cardboard, and on top of other paints and hard surfaces, such as wood. Wash brushes in water before the paint dries.
Poster paint is easy to use and brushes can be washed in water when you finish.
Buy these in an art or toy shop.
Paint means house paint. Wash brushes in **white spirit** if you use gloss house paint, but in water if you use emulsion paint.
Varnish is used to give surfaces a long-lasting, shiny finish. Polyurethane varnish is best. Wash brushes in white spirit.
You can buy these in a hardware or do-it-yourself shop.

Fasteners

Map pins are short pins with small, round, coloured heads.
Drawing-pins are stronger and have big heads.
Paper clips hold pieces of light-weight paper or card together.
Paper fasteners have two prongs which you push through paper or cardboard, then bend outward.
Pins are ordinary straight ones.
Safety-pins are ones with a catch. Buy these from a stationer's shop.
Staple pins are three-sided metal fasteners used for holding wire mesh to a frame.
Corrugated fasteners are pieces of ridged metal which hold joints of wood together.
Buy these last two kinds at a hardware or do-it-yourself shop.

Glues and tapes

Buy these at a stationer's, do-it-yourself or hardware shop.

Glue means any ordinary glue, such as paper paste, that will stick paper and thin cardboard.

Strong glue means Bostik, UHU or Araldite, for sticking heavier materials together.

Wood glue sticks wood together.

PVA is a white glue used for sticking cloth, beads, braid or wool to other surfaces.

Masking tape is used to stick things to walls or windows without leaving marks. Don't fix it too firmly and avoid paper surfaces.

Sewing things

These may be bought in the haberdashery department of a store or in a handicraft shop.

Knitting needles are the ones used for making woollen clothes.

Darning needles have big eyes to take wool and are sharp.

Tapestry needles also have big eyes, but are blunt.

Cheesecloth and muslin are very fine, net-like cloths.

Embroidery thread is usually thicker and shiny.

Shirring elastic is very thin.

Dressmaker's chalk is used for marking cloth.

Wood

You can buy most kinds of wood in a hardware or do-it-yourself shop.

Plywood is made up of layers of wood glued together.

Exterior plywood has a special surface finish so that it can be left out-of-doors.

Softwood is inexpensive and nails and screws go into it easily.

Beading is a thin strip of wood with one rounded side.

Dowelling is always round.

Bamboo and cane rods are very light. Buy them at a gardening centre or plant shop.

Wire

Wire mesh is made up of strands of wire woven together like a net.

Galvanised wire is the kind that doesn't rust.

Buy these at a hardware or do-it-yourself shop.

Electrical wire has a plastic cover.

Fuse wire is fine metal thread. Buy these at an electrical shop.

Garden wire is usually green. Buy it at a garden centre or plant shop.

Other things

Plaster of Paris is a powder that sets hard when mixed with water and left (the drying time will vary according to how much is used and whether the air is dry or damp). *Never pour left-over plaster down the sink.*

Self-hardening clay also sets hard. Don't put it in a warm place to hurry it up as the edges will curl. You will have to work fast with this clay or it will set before you are ready.

Plasticine can be reused. Buy these in a craft or toy shop.

Magnets can be bought in a hardware or toy shop.

Bulb, bulb holder, battery can all be bought in an electrical shop.

Basic shapes

You'll find an introduction to basic, flat shapes round the edges of these pages – and hints on how to make them three-dimensional.

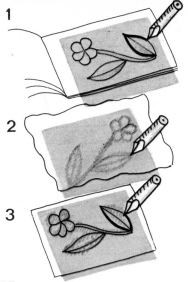

How to trace

1. Put the paper over the trace pattern on the page of the book and draw the outline of the pattern on it.
2. Turn the tracing paper over and put it on a piece of **scrap paper.** Scribble over the outline.
3. Put the tracing right side up, on a **clean sheet of paper,** and draw round the outline again.

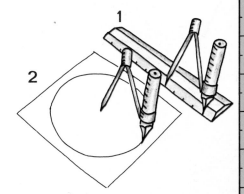

Drawing a circle

1. Set the arms of a **pair of compasses** against a **ruler** and measure the distance of the radius of the circle you want.
2. Put the pin arm on the **paper or cardboard** to mark the centre of the circle.

Swing the **pencil** arm round to draw a complete circle.

Make things move

Turn a **drinking straw** into a magic wand.
1. Dip one end of the straw in some **sugar.**
Use a **cloth** to wipe the sugar off the outside of the straw.
2. Dip the other end of the straw in **soft soap.**
Wipe the straw again so the soap can't be seen.

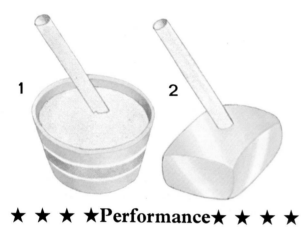

★ ★ ★ ★Performance★ ★ ★ ★

Now show your friends how you can make two matchsticks move without touching them.
3. Put **two dead matchsticks** in **water.**
4. Dip the sugared end of the straw into the water between the matches.
The matches will move close together.
5. Dip in the soapy end of the straw.
The matches will move apart.

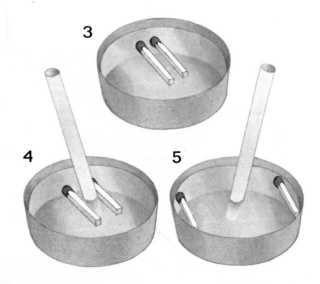

Watermark wizard

Make someone's name appear as if by magic.
1. Soak a sheet of **paper** in **water,** then put the wet paper on a **mirror or window.**
2. Put a dry sheet of paper over the wet one.
3. With a **pencil,** write the name of your best friend on the top sheet of paper.
4. Throw the *top sheet* away and leave the bottom sheet of paper to dry.
The name on the paper will then be invisible.

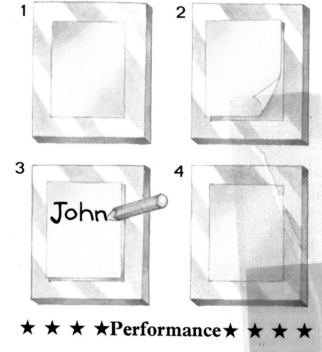

★ ★ ★ ★Performance★ ★ ★ ★

5. Hold up the sheet of paper and say that you can make your friend's name appear on it.
6. Put the paper in a **bowl of water** and the writing will show up.

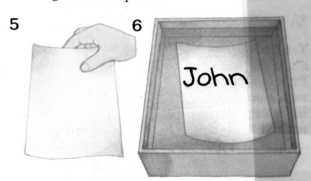

Tube of plenty

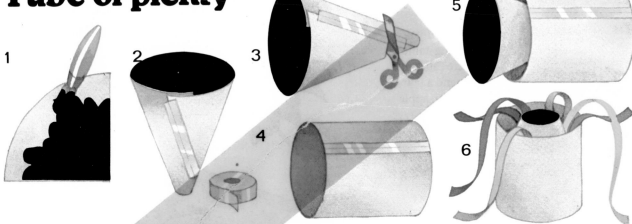

1

2

3

4

5

6

Make ribbons appear from nowhere! With **scissors,** cut a curve on a sheet of **thin card** 20 cm square.
1. Paint the shape with **black poster paint.** Let the paint dry. Fold the cardboard into a cone with the black surface inside.
2. Put **sticky tape** on the join.

3. Cut off the tip of the cone. Cut another sheet of cardboard about 27cm by 16cm.
4. Fold the cardboard into a tube and put sticky tape on the join. The widest end of the cone should just fit inside the tube.

5. Use **glue** to fix the top edges of the cone and tube together.
6. When the glue is dry put some **coloured ribbons** in the space between the cone and the tube.

★ ★ ★ ★ ★ ★ ★ ★ ★ ★ **Performance** ★ ★ ★ ★ ★ ★ ★ ★ ★ ★ ★

Hold the tube so that the ribbons face you.
7. Show everyone the other end of the tube. It will look empty. Now put the tube down on a **table.**
8. Say, 'Hey presto!' Then pull out the ribbons – one by one.

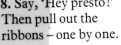

7

8

Inviting visitors

Making friends with small birds is easy if you give them a place to bathe and a feeding-table in your garden. Hang the table where cats can't get to it. Every day, leave out water and a few fresh scraps – bread, bacon rind, cheese, apple cores – or some bird seed. Put water in a heavy bowl with a thick rim. Hang up half a coconut shell, if you can get one. Clean the table with a brush, sweeping out at the corners.

Bird table
Ask an adult to help you. Buy a 25cm-square piece of **exterior plywood,** four pieces of **wooden beading** 21cm by 1cm, **wood glue, four nails** and some **fine, strong cord.**
1. Glue the beading to the edges of the table top so that gaps are left at each corner.
Use a **hammer** to fix a nail into the table at all four corners, leaving the heads sticking up.
2. Firmly tie a length of cord to each nail, then wind the lengths round the **branch of a tree.**

Bird bath
With a **spade,** dig a shallow hole in a quiet, sunny part of the garden. Use **plastic** to line the hole, and put **stones** round the edge to keep it in place. Or simply sink a shallow dish into the hole. Fill the bath with **water** and watch how the birds play and splash about in it.

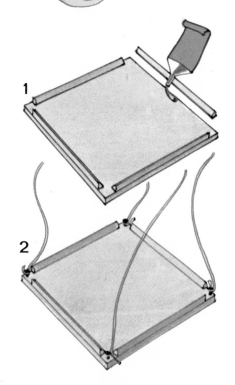

Feathery fliers

After birds have been visiting, collect their fallen feathers, and make a mobile with them.
1. With **tracing paper** and a **pencil,** trace this little bird. Use **scissors** to cut out five birds from **coloured cardboard.**
Paint eyes on each one with **poster paint** and a **brush** and stick **feathers** on with **glue.** Make a tiny hole in each bird and tie on varying lengths of **cotton thread.**
2. Loosely tie the birds to **two bamboo or cane rods** – one 30cm long and one 23cm long – as shown. Tie thread to the top rod and hang up your mobile. Now slide the loose knots to and fro until the birds are perfectly balanced. Fix the knots into place by dabbing them with **nail polish.** Trim off any spare thread.

Who goes there?

Find out which animals live in your area by taking plaster casts of their footprints. Search near rivers and ponds for tracks. Take a **bucket, wooden spoon, water, plaster of Paris, cardboard strips** 60cm by 6cm, **paper clips.**

Join the ends of one cardboard strip with a paper clip.
1. Press the cardboard circle into the earth, surrounding the track. Pour water into the bucket and slowly stir in plaster until the mixture is like custard.
2. Gently pour the plaster into the circle to a depth of 2.5cm. Leave it for two hours to dry. Carefully lift up the cardboard with the plaster cast inside.
3. At home, remove the cardboard. Clean off any mud with a **brush.** Look in an **animal book** if you don't recognise the footprint.

Tin can trotters

Find **two empty cans** with press-on lids (chocolate or syrup cans). Remove the lids – you will not need them.
1. Ask an adult to punch two holes through the bottom of each can using a **hammer** and **nail.**
2. Thread a piece of **string** 1 metre long down through one of the holes in one can and up through the other. Tie the ends of the string together. Thread the second can in the same way. Stand with one foot on each can and hold the long loops of string in your hands. Now see how well you can trot!

Whizzer

Turn spots into rings of colour.
1. With a **pencil** draw round an up-turned **teacup** *once* on **stiff cardboard** and *twice* on **white paper**. Cut out the circles with **scissors**.
2. Use **glue** to stick a paper circle to each side of the cardboard.
3. With the point of the scissors make two holes 1.5cm apart as shown.
4. Thread a piece of **string** 1.5 metres long through the holes and tie the ends.
5. Paint spots of red, yellow and blue **poster paint** on both sides of the whizzer as shown. Leave to dry.
Flick the whizzer over and over to wind it up. Pull the string to make it whizz.

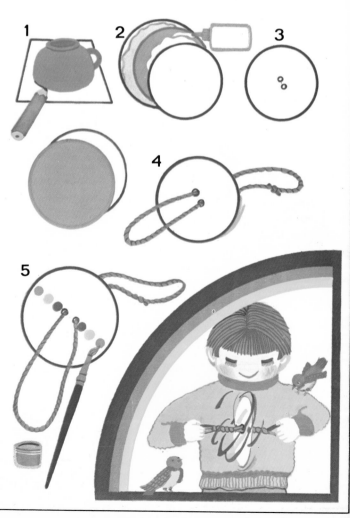

Pierrot puppet

Make a cheerful puppet on a rainy indoor day.
Cut legs and arms from **scraps of felt** with **scissors**.
Trace the pattern for the head on to **card** and cut it out.
Draw a face on it with **felt-tipped pens.**
Fix the arms, legs and head to a **matchbox** with **sticky tape.**
Stick a strip of **coloured paper** all round the matchbox with **glue.**
Cut dots of felt for pompons and glue them on.
Cut three pieces of **shirring elastic** about 30cm long.
Attach one to each hand and one to the top of the hat.
Tie the other ends to a strip of card.

trace pattern

Bounce Pierrot from the card to make him dance.

A wind vane

Meteorologists, or weather men, use wind vanes to observe changes in the direction of the wind. You can make one for yourself.

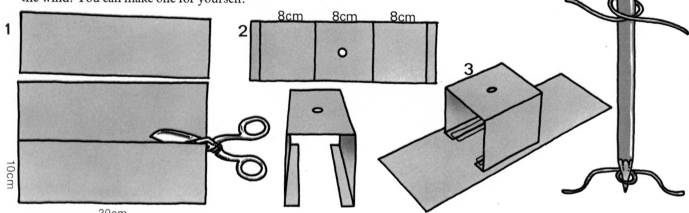

1. Use **scissors** to cut three pieces of **cardboard,** each 30cm by 10cm.

2. With the tip of the scissors, score across one piece of cardboard at the points shown. Make a hole in the middle with the scissors. Push a **pencil** through it until the hole is just a little bigger than the pencil. Bend the cardboard along the scored lines.

3. Use **sticky tape** to fix the folded card to one of the other pieces of cardboard. This is the stand for the wind vane. Now straighten **two paper clips.**

4. Wrap one paper clip loosely round the top of the pencil, and the other one loosely round the sharpened end. Take the paper clips off the pencil.

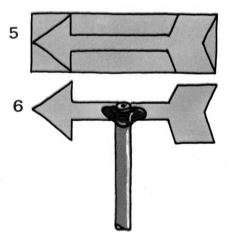

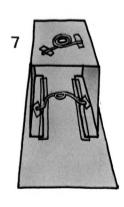

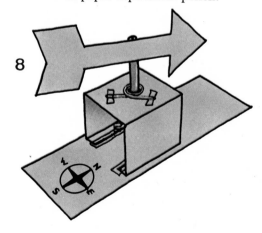

5. Draw an arrow, like the one shown, on the third piece of cardboard. Cut out the shape.

6. Use **plasticine** to fix the pencil to the centre of the arrow. Make sure you use an equal amount of plasticine on both sides of the pencil, or the arrow won't balance properly.

7. Use sticky tape to fix one paper clip over the hole in the stand. Fix the other one to the base, directly underneath. Stand the pencil in the hole.

8. Mark the points of the compass on the base. Outside, point the base so that 'E' faces the direction of the rising sun. Record the direction of the wind each day.

Record wind speed

To see how fast or slow the wind blows, make an *anenometer* – a wind speed measurer.

You will need **stiff cardboard** 60cm by 30cm.

1. Measure four 15cm widths with a **ruler,** and draw **pencil** lines across these points.

Score down the lines with **scissors.**

2. Set a **pair of compasses** to 10cm and draw an arc on the cardboard as shown.

Cut out a narrow slot along the arc.

Mark numbers at equal intervals along the slot.

Fold the cardboard inwards along the scored lines. Put **sticky tape** along the two edges and along all the folded edges.

3. Cut a piece of **paper** 12cm square and tape it to the end of the box as shown.

Take the anenometer outside and point the flap towards the wind. Each night and morning, record the level that the flap reaches.

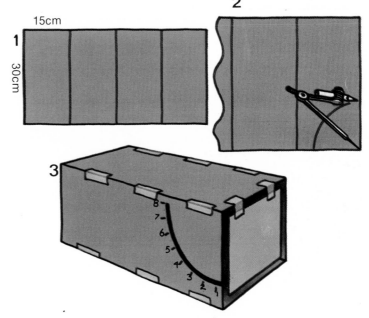

Measure the rain

Keep a record of the amount of rain that falls by using a simple measuring device.

Find **four empty glass jars.** They must have straight sides and all be the same size.

Put the jars outside and wait for it to rain.

Leave the jars to collect water over a 24-hour period.

Now pour all the water you've collected into just *one* of the jars.

Use a **ruler** to measure the water's depth. Divide the depth by the number of jars. For instance, if the water measures 2cm the sum will be $\frac{2}{4}$ (or $\frac{1}{2}$), which means that 0.50cm of rain has fallen.

Consequences

In this game nobody wins or loses but everyone will laugh when it is finished. Two or more people can play the game.

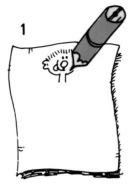

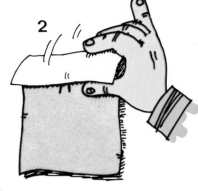

Each player needs **paper** and a **pencil**.
1. At the top of the paper each player draws the head of a person or animal. The head must have a long neck drawn on it.

2. Each player folds over the paper so that only the neck shows. Then the folded paper is passed on to the next player.

Five stones

This is a game to play when you're all on your own and you want to amuse yourself.

Five Stones is an old game, and there are many ways to play it. The Ancient Greeks played it with the ankle bones of sheep. You need **five stones** (obviously!) but practise with three until you are good at the game.

Put the five (or three) stones in the palm of your hand. Throw the stones into the air. Now, turn your hand over, spread your fingers as wide as possible, and try to catch all the stones on the back of your hand as they fall.

Or hold one stone in your hand and space the other four on the ground. Throw the one stone into the air and, before catching it, pick up one stone from the ground. Do the same, trying to pick up two stones, then three, then all four.

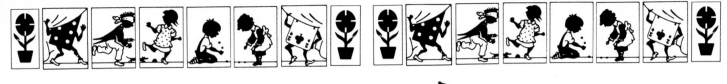

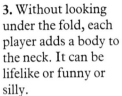

3 **4**

3. Without looking under the fold, each player adds a body to the neck. It can be lifelike or funny or silly.
The papers are folded and passed on again.

4. Finally, draw legs and feet, and pass on the papers as before. Now unfold the papers. Who's got the funniest or strangest 'human-animal'? Can anyone give it a name?

 **1 5**

Pick-a-stick

Toys and games shops sell special sticks for playing this game but ordinary **lolly and ice-cream sticks** work just as well.

Ask all your friends to save their lolly and ice-cream sticks for you. Wash the sticks and leave them to dry. You will need about 30. Play the game on your own, or challenge one of your friends to play with you.

Each player chooses one stick as a 'playing stick'.
The rest of the sticks are held in an upright bunch by one player. This player then lets all the sticks fall in a heap on the floor or table.

The first player uses his playing stick to lift one stick from the heap. He mustn't make any other stick move. If he does, then it's the other player's turn.
The player who lifts off the most sticks is the winner.

A friendly file

The police keep records of photographs and fingerprints to identify people. Here's an 'identity' file with a cheerful difference: a collection of lip and fingerprints on cards. Ask your friends and family if they would like to be included in your special file. Then make cards all the same size by cutting up **thin cardboard** with **scissors**. Use a **pencil or pen** to write in a person's name, address, birthday, colour of hair and eyes, height and weight, or hobbies. Paste on a photograph if you have one. Ask someone to lend you an **old lipstick**. Rub the lipstick on a friend's finger and press the finger firmly on that person's card. Do the same with lips and ask everyone to 'kiss' their personal card.

For a file, use a **box or ribbon.** Punch a hole in each card to thread ribbon through.

Alphabet letters

Have you ever noticed how many different kinds of **letters** there are ? Look at the variety of letters printed in books, magazines and newspapers or on advertisements, labels and greeting cards. Each kind of letter has its own name. For instance, the ordinary upright type – like the words printed here – is called roman. Slanting type (*like this*) is called italic.
Use **scissors** to cut out letters. *(Don't cut up books.)* Find as many different A's, B's and so on, as possible, and use **glue** to fix them in a **scrapbook.** You could have a page for each letter of the alphabet.
Or glue down your letters so that they make pictures. You could use them to design animals like this one, or houses, or people.

Money, money, money

Collect coins instead of spending them! Save up your own money or go on a treasure hunt for lost coins. (Make sure the coins you find don't belong to someone else.) Search under chair cushions, between floorboards, or behind dusty shelves. Ask if you can dig in the garden for lost or buried coins. Or ask travelling friends or relatives for their spare foreign coins.

If the coins you find are dirty, wash them in **warm, soapy water** or soak them in a solution of **salt and vinegar.** Don't use metal polish to clean them as this will wear away the design. You could display your favourite coins in a special clay box. Cover them with plastic if you like. If you have extra coins, why not make a money paperweight?

Display box

1. Use a **rolling pin** to roll some **self-hardening clay** into a square or oblong shape. The clay should be about 2cm thick.

2. Make sure the top is very flat and even, then trim the edges of the clay with an **old kitchen knife** so that they are neat.

3. Press the **coins** into the clay until they are level with the top of it. Then carefully lift all the coins out.

4. Leave the clay to harden. Don't put it in a warm place or it will curl up. When the clay is hard, arrange your coins for display.

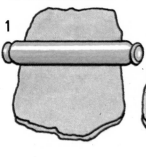

1

2

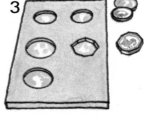

3

4

Coin paperweight

1. Pile up a handful of **coins.** Choose the sort that you have two or more of in your collection.

2. Use **scissors** to cut a piece of **stiff cardboard** into a base for your paperweight. It can be any shape.

3. Cover the top of the cardboard with **strong glue,** and press down a layer of coins very close together.

4. Glue on more coins to make a pile. Trim off any cardboard that shows. Put **varnish** on the coins with a **brush.**

1

2

3

4

Count the cats

Can you see cats in this picture ? Altogether there are 25 – some are huge and some are very tiny and a few are upside down.

The tricky 'T'

Use **pencil** to trace these shapes on to **tracing paper,** then use the pattern and **scissors** to cut out the shapes in **cardboard.** Number them, and keep all the numbered sides facing you.

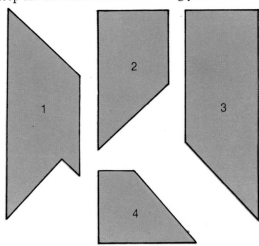

The four pieces fit together in a certain way to make a capital 'T'. See if you can do it.

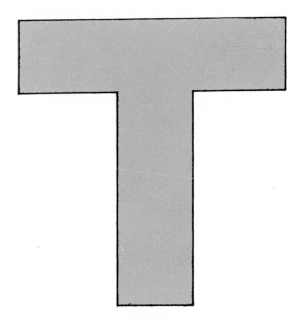

This 'T' is exactly the same size as the puzzle pieces when they're put together properly.
(The solution is in the back of the book.)

Solve the problem

A man is going to the market to sell a fox, a hen and some grain. He has to cross a river and his boat is just big enough to hold himself and one other thing.

When he gets to the river he finds he has a problem. If he leaves the fox with the hen, the hen will be eaten by the fox. He can't leave the hen and the grain together, because the hen will feast itself on the grain. Only the fox and the grain can be left safely together. How does the man get all three and himself across the river?

(You might have to think for a long time about this problem. Check your solution by looking at the pages of Answers in the back of the book.)

From one to nine

In these boxes the numbers placed diagonally (2,5,8) add up to 15. Can you arrange the rest of the numbers between one and nine (1,3,4,6,7, 9) so that the numbers add up to 15 in every direction? Add up all the rows of numbers from left to right and from top to bottom and the other diagonal row.

(Look in the back of the book for the answer.)

Finger pictures

Here's a clever way of making pictures without using crayons or brushes.
Pour some **poster paint** on to a **sponge.** Mix it with a little **water** if necessary, but do not make it too runny.

Press your finger first on to the sponge and then on to a clean sheet of **paper.** Experiment with your other fingers, the side of your hand or even your whole hand to make all kinds of pictures.

Here are some shapes to try:

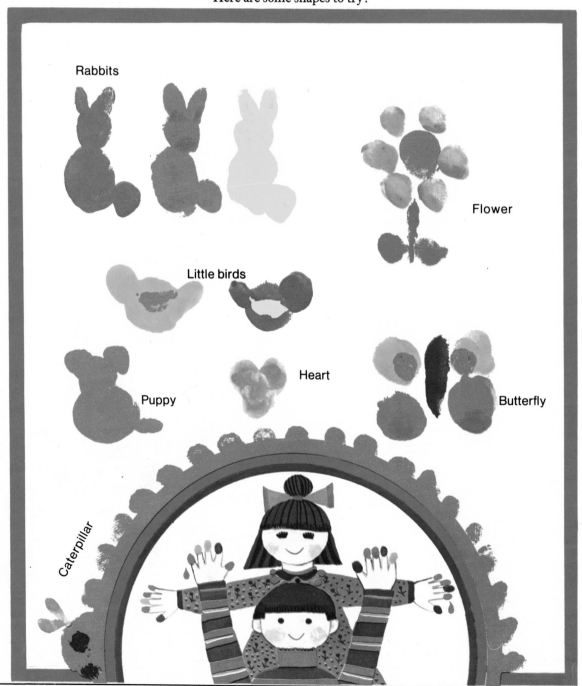

Rabbits

Flower

Little birds

Puppy

Heart

Butterfly

Caterpillar

Magazine collage

Look through some **old magazines** and rip out the patches of plain colour. Sort out the different colours into piles. Tear or cut up the pieces of paper as you use them.

Use **glue** to stick the pieces down on a sheet of **paper** to make a picture. Think how you can use light and dark shades of the same colour. Use dark shades for shadows, for instance.

Predict the card

This special bag will help you 'predict' which card will be chosen from a whole **pack of cards.**
1. Use **sticky tape** to fix a **sheet of paper** into a **paper bag** so that it makes two compartments.
2. Put a playing card in one side of the bag. With a **pencil,** write the name of the card on **a slip of paper.** Put it in the same compartment.

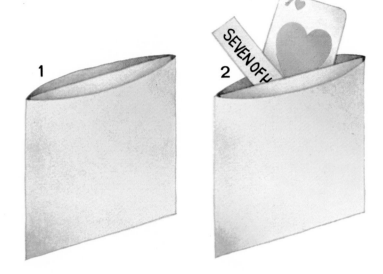

★ ★ ★ ★ ★ ★ ★ ★ ★ ★ ★ ★ **Performance** ★ ★ ★ ★ ★ ★ ★ ★ ★ ★ ★ ★ ★

Show everyone the 'ordinary' bag.
3. Pretend to write the name of a card on **another slip of paper.** Put the slip into the *empty* compartment of the paper bag.
4. Spread all the cards face down and ask someone to touch any card.

5. Put the touched card into the same compartment of the bag as the blank paper slip.
Hold the secret divider against the other side of the bag.
6. Tip the bag up so that the card and paper slip you put in secretly will drop out.
7. Ask someone to read your prediction and show the card. They will be a perfect match! (Don't let anyone see that there is still a card and slip of paper in the bag.)

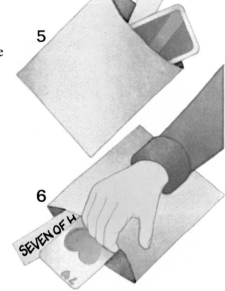

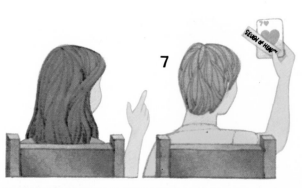

Robot ball

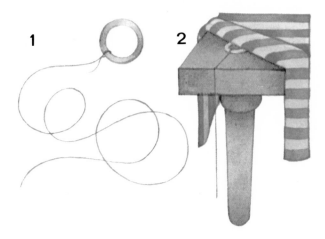

1

2

Ask a friend to help you do this magic trick.
1. Tie a long piece of **cotton thread** to a **curtain ring.**
Put the ring on a **table** with the thread hanging over the edge.
2. Cover the table with a **cloth.**

Performance

Tell your audience you can command a ball to move of its own accord.
Put a **small ball** on the hidden ring.
3. At your command, your friend pulls the thread hanging under the tablecloth.
The ball will then roll across the table.

3

Scratch it out

Here is a different trick of movement that will surprise your friends.
Put **two big coins** on a **tablecloth,** then put a **smaller coin** between them.
1. Turn a **glass tumbler** upside down so that its rim rests on the two big coins.
Ask someone to try to get the smaller coin out without touching the glass or any of the coins.
When the person gives up, you can show how easily it is done.
2. Keep scratching the tablecloth in front of the glass. Gradually, the smaller coin will move out from under the glass.

1

2

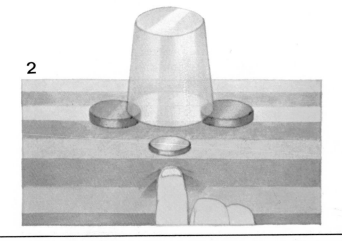

Take a peek!

Imagine being able to watch wild animals eating
or sleeping or playing right before your eyes.
It's very difficult to do this out of doors,
but you can observe animals any time you like
through the glass wall of a *vivarium*. Vivarium
is the proper word for a container in which you
raise small animals in surroundings where they
feel at home. Use a fish tank or **ask an adult**
to help you make a vivarium out of a box.
You will need a **strong wooden box** 60cm long,
50cm wide, and 50cm deep. Look for a box in
second-hand or junk shops, or **ask an adult** to
build a three-sided one for you. Make sure
there are no gaps in your box.
Buy from a hardware or do-it-yourself shop:
160cm of **plastic channelling**; a piece of **glass**
60cm by 50cm; two pieces of **softwood** 60cm long
and 3cm thick and two more pieces 44cm long by
3cm; **four corrugated fasteners**; a tube of **wood
glue**; a piece of **wire mesh** 60cm by 50cm; a box
of **staple pins**; a piece of **plastic or polythene**
64cm by 54cm; **paint** and a **paintbrush**.

1. Take off one long
side of the box by
knocking against it
with a **hammer.**
Put several coats of
paint on the inside.
Let the paint dry.
2. Fit the plastic
channelling along the
open side and slot the
glass into it.
3. Glue the pieces of
softwood together as a
frame for the top.

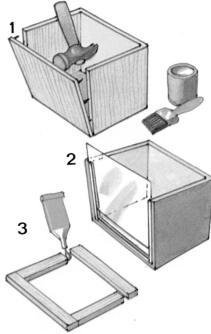

4. Hammer a corrugated
fastener across each
joint of the frame to
hold it firmly.
5. Stretch the wire
mesh over the frame
and fix it into place
with staple pins.
6. Line the floor with
the plastic or
polythene so that 4cm
is turned up against
the side of the box to
hold the soil.

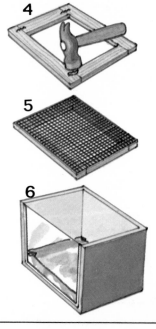

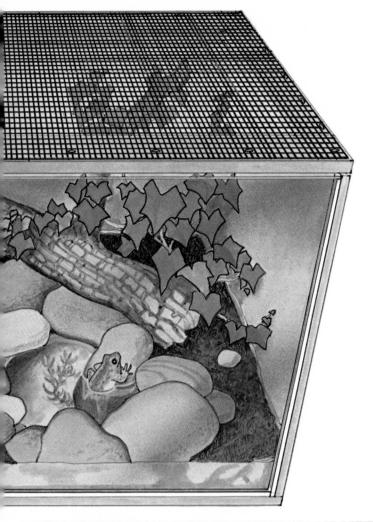

Choosing an animal

You could raise frogs and toads in the vivarium; or lizards; or a terrapin – a kind of tortoise. Pet shops sell all these. Read some books about the conditions and food an animal likes before you decide to raise one.

Decorating its 'home'

Look at the chart below to see what kind of **soil, plants** and other things you should put into the vivarium for the animal you have chosen. You can make a pond by sinking a **bowl** into the soil, then filling it with **water.**
Slope the soil away from the pond and surround it with **stones.** Put plants directly into the soil, or grow them in pots and then sink these into the soil. Plants should be growing well before you put an animal into the vivarium.

Catching the food

Look under stones or logs in your garden, or in woods and parks for worms. Catch insects in a butterfly net (Project 132). Sweep the net through bushes and undergrowth to catch them. Because there are different *species* (or types) of animals, you may have to experiment with food to see which sort your animal likes best. Always put dead food in a bowl, and make sure the pond has fresh water all the time.

Animals	Soil	Plants	Conditions	Food
Frogs and toads	Moist soil mixed with peat.	Swiss cheese plant and pond weeds.	Small pond with rock in it for sitting on. Keep the vivarium in a shady place all the time.	All insects; worms and mealworms. Feed once or twice a week.
Lizards	Dry soil mixed with gravel and sand.	Sweetheart plant and ivy. Dry bracken or heather to scratch dead skin against.	Rocks; sticks or branches. Put the vivarium in a warm spot for a few hours each day.	Live insects. Feed about twice a week.
Terrapin	Gravelly soil mixed with peat.	Moss, ivy and pond weeds.	Rocks and bark. Pond (half the size of the box) to rest in. Put the vivarium in a warm spot each day.	Live worms and insects; raw fish or meat. Feed three times a week.

Sausages

The faster you play this game and the more people playing it, the funnier it is.

Choose one player to be 'It'.
All the other players take it in turns to ask 'It' a question. Ask anything you wish – it could be, 'What's your name?', 'Who is your best friend?' or 'What is your teacher like?'.
Whatever the question, 'It' must always answer, 'Sausages!' – without laughing.
If 'It' laughs, he is out and someone else is chosen to be 'It'.
You'll probably find that nobody (including 'It') can stop laughing!

Slowcoach

Think like a snail because in this race the player who comes last is the winner!

Mark out a short distance for the 'race-track'. Line all the players up on the track. When the starter says, 'Go!' everyone moves off as *slowly* as possible. Anyone who stops completely is out. The last player across the finishing line wins.

Sniffies

Next time you have a party, play this game with all your guests. Identifying things by smell is not easy, but it's amusing to try. See how many correct guesses everyone makes.

You need a **pencil, paper** and a **blindfold** for each guest, **four saucers** and **four things to sniff.**
Choose things with a strong smell – curry powder, cocoa, coffee, lemon peel or washing-up liquid. (**Ask an adult** for these things.)
Put one thing in each saucer secretly.
Blindfold all the guests and bring in the saucers. Warn them to sniff *gently*, then each player takes it in turn to sniff. Then take all the saucers away, and ask the players to write down their four guesses.
The player with most correct answers wins.

You can play a different version of this game by trying to identify things by the way they *feel*.
All the players must be blindfolded. A **few objects** are put into an **old pillowcase or sack.** These could be a feather, a piece of rubber, something woolly or silky, a scrap of felt or a piece of fruit such as a banana or an apple.
Everyone plays the game as 'Sniffies' is played, except they feel instead of smelling.

Guess how I do it

This is an acting and guessing game. You don't need to be a good actor and your guesses might be wild ones, but the game is fun to play.
Two people or a whole group can play it.

One player is chosen to leave the room. He is the guesser.
The others pick an *adverb* (a word describing how something is done). It might be 'angrily', 'cunningly', 'stupidly', or some other word.
When everyone is ready, the guesser comes in and commands one of the players to act the word by performing a task. He might say, 'Clean your teeth!' or 'Walk across the room!'. The player must do whatever the guesser asks in a way that describes the chosen word.
If the guesser can't tell what the word is, he can ask another player to act a different task.
When the guesser gets the right answer, somebody else becomes the guesser, and another word is chosen by the rest of the players.

Interruptions

Ask someone in your family to play a word game with you if a rainy day keeps you all indoors.

You will need a **newspaper or a magazine.**
Decide to be someone who sells things – say, a greengrocer, a butcher, or a sweet shop owner. Your partner has to read from the newspaper or magazine, missing out all the *nouns* (the words that name things). Whenever there is a pause, you call out the name of something you sell. The most boring piece of news suddenly becomes very funny when you fill it with 'bananas' or 'pig's trotters' and so on!

Constantinople

Here is another word game you can save for a wintry or rainy day.

You will need **pencils, paper, a clock** and two or more players.
Choose a long word – one with at least ten letters in it. (Look in a **dictionary** or ask an adult if you can't think of one.)
Each player writes down smaller words, using any of the letters in the long word. The words must not be *proper nouns* (names of people or places) and they should have three or more letters in them. (Check words in a dictionary.)
The player with the most words wins.
Now, go! You have five minutes to play.

String telephone

Ring up a friend on a home-made 'telephone'.
Cut two strips of **paper,** each 80cm by 10cm.
1. Roll each strip into a cylinder about 10cm
in diameter. Fix the joins with **sticky tape.**
Put each cylinder on **cardboard** 20cm by 10cm.
2. Draw round the cylinders with a **pencil,** and
use **scissors** to cut out the two circles.
Make a small hole in the centre of each circle.
3. Tape one circle to the end of each cylinder.
4. Thread one end of a long piece of **string**
through each hole. Tie big knots in the ends.
Keep the string taut when you 'telephone'.
String carries sound better than air does.

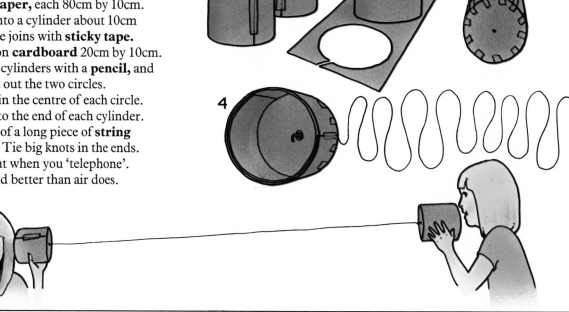

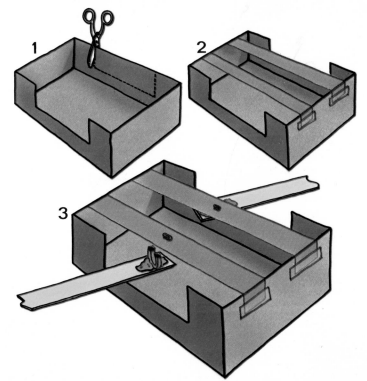

Magnet race-track

See how magnets work (they attract most metal
objects containing iron) and have fun, too.
1. Using **scissors,** cut out the bottom and sides
of a **box** as shown.
Cut two 4cm-wide **cardboard** strips longer than
the box. (Don't use really thick cardboard.)
2. Fix the strips to the box with **sticky tape.**
Now you need **two rulers** and **two magnets.**
Put a lump of **plasticine** on the end of each ruler
and press a magnet into each lump.
Get **two paper clips** and put one on the end of
each track. A player must try to get his paper
clip to the end of the track by using the force
of the magnet. (Steady hands are needed!)
3. Hold the magnets below the tracks.
If a player's magnet touches the track or his
paper clip falls off, he must start again.

Stand-up clown

An egg-shell will stand upright if you weight it. Dress it as a clown and watch it move!

1. Gently mould a lump of **plasticine** into the bottom of an **egg-shell.**

Cut a strip of **paper** about 20cm by 8cm. Roll it into a cylinder the same size as the top of the shell. Join the edges with **sticky tape.**

2. Tape the cylinder to the top of the shell. Use a **pair of compasses** to draw a 10cm-diameter circle on paper. Cut it out with scissors.

3. Cut from the circle's edge to its centre. Twist the circle into a cone shape and put sticky tape on the join.

Tape the cone to the paper cylinder to make a hat. Paint the clown with **poster colours.**

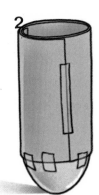

Soil settling jar

Soil is a mixture of different particles. It could include sand, clay, peat and gravel, though you may not be able to see them all. If you put soil into a **glass jar with a lid,** you will be able to see the different parts. Use an **old spoon** to dig up a little **soil** from various places in a garden.

1. Half fill the jar with the different soils.

2. Fill the jar with **water.** Screw on the lid. Shake the jar well, and then leave it to stand. The soil will separate into layers – the heaviest part of the soil will settle on the bottom and the lightest will rest on top.

Going international

Modern postcards are easy to collect because they are sold all over the world. Buy them when you are on holiday or ask friends and relatives to send you postcards if they go abroad.
There are thousands of cards that show views of places or buildings. But there are many other kinds, too. You could look for postcards that show birds, animals or flowers, or ones that illustrate a joke. Or collect postcards of famous paintings from art galleries and museums. If you decide to collect old postcards, search in junk shops and second-hand bookshops for really cheap ones.

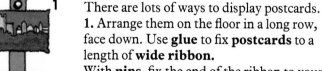

There are lots of ways to display postcards.
1. Arrange them on the floor in a long row, face down. Use **glue** to fix **postcards** to a length of **wide ribbon.**
With **pins,** fix the end of the ribbon to your bedroom door or to a picture rail.
2. Decorate a **table top** with a collage of **postcards.** They will stay in place if you cover them with a sheet of **glass. Ask an adult** to help you get glass cut to the right size.
3. Keep your **postcards** in a traditional **album.** Mount them with **transparent photographic hinges** so that you can see every bit of each card.

2

1
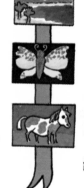

3

Postcard cubes
Cut a piece of **paper** 40cm by 30cm.
1. With a **pencil** and **ruler,** draw on it six squares, each measuring 9cm, and seven tabs as shown.

Use **scissors** to cut up **postcards** into 9cm squares.
2. Glue the postcard squares to the paper squares.

When the **glue** is dry, fold the paper into a cube.
3. Spread glue on the tabs and stick them together.

1

2

3
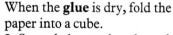

Make as many cubes as you like by repeating steps 1-3.
Pile the cubes up to make an attractive group of pictures.

When your pile topples over, give your extra cubes away as Christmas or birthday presents.

As sweet as sugar

When you go to a restaurant or cafe, look out for **wrapped-up sugar lumps or** little **printed packets of sugar.** Ask the waiter or the owner if you can have some for your collection. You might also see specially-packed sugar at airports or in hotels and theatres.

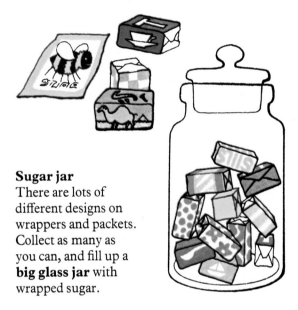

Sugar jar
There are lots of different designs on wrappers and packets. Collect as many as you can, and fill up a **big glass jar** with wrapped sugar.

Wrapper diary
Use **glue** to stick **empty wrappers** into a **diary or notebook.** With a **pencil or pen,** write next to each one the place where you collected it, the date, who went with you, what you ate, and if anything special happened.

Beads all in a row

Beads are lovely things to collect because they come in so many different colours, materials, shapes and sizes. Ask your mother (or an aunt or grandmother) if she has any beads from a broken necklace. Or buy beads in charity shops, craft and hobby shops or jumble sales.
You could collect glass beads or wooden ones, or beads of all kinds. String them on a length of thin cord to make a necklace. Or **ask an adult** to help you display them in a frame.

Bead picture
1. Use a **hammer** to put **nails** into the sides of an **old picture frame.** Space them evenly on both sides and leave the heads sticking up a bit.

Tie a piece of **thin string** to one nail.
2. Thread **beads** on it, and tie the end of the string to the opposite nail. Dab the knots with **strong glue.**

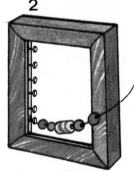

3. Continue threading beads on lengths of string for each pair of nails.
Hang the frame on your bedroom wall for everyone to admire.

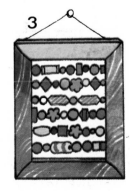

Which way to go?

Imagine you are walking down a road from a little town. You're on your way to visit someone in another town.

After a mile or so, you reach some crossroads. Here there should be a sign-post pointing in all four directions, naming the town at the end of each of the four roads. The sign-post is there, but it has fallen over. Its four pointers are still attached to it.

How do you know which road to take? There is no one to ask and you can't see any of the towns in the distance.

(There is a very simple solution, and it is given in the back of the book.)

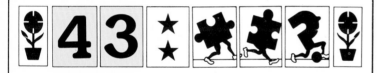

Two-way envelope

Can you draw this 'envelope' without taking your **pencil** off the **paper**? The only rule is that you mustn't go back along any line you've already drawn.

A clue: there are two places where you could start drawing, so there are two solutions to this puzzle.

(The answers are in the back of the book.)

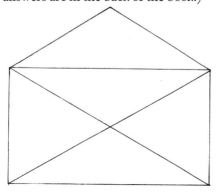

Odds and evens

Some of the cars in this picture are identical in everything except colour. But some are odd because they don't match any other car.

Count up the pairs that match each other. How many odd ones are left?
(The answer is in the back of the book.)

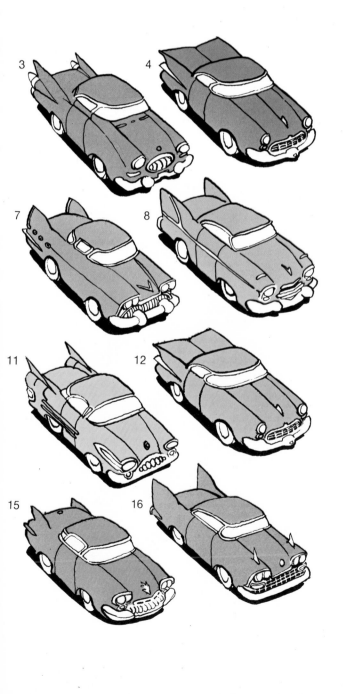

'Korshinodoniger'

This weird creature with the imaginary name is made up of parts of six real animals. See if you can identify each one of them.
(All six animals are listed on the pages of Answers in the back of the book.)

Lots of triangles

There are 35 triangles in this *pentagon* (five-sided figure). Can you find them all?
(Look in the back of the book for the answer.)

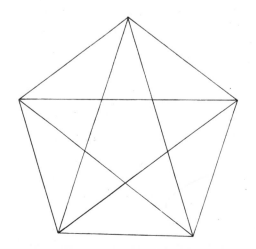

Squirmy wormery

Worms live underground where you can't see, but you can watch them at home in a wormery.

Find a **large empty jar.** You won't need a lid. Put in a layer of **damp soil.** Add a layer of **sand.** Then fill the jar with more damp soil.

With a **spade,** dig up a patch of earth to find **two or three worms.** Collect a **few leaves,** too.

1. Put the worms and leaves on top of the soil. Stretch a piece of **cheesecloth** over the jar and hold it in place with a **rubber band.**

2. Wrap **black paper** round the jar and fix the joins with **sticky tape.**

Leave the jar for a few days.

3. Take the paper off. See how the burrowing worms have mingled the soil and sand?

To keep worms as pets, make sure that they always have fresh leaves and moist soil.

Fruit fancy

Here's a way to make sure that everyone knows which fruit is yours – initial it.

Use **scissors** to cut out your initials from a sheet of **black paper.**

Mix **flour** and **water** in a **bowl** to make a paste. Put some paste on one side of the initials and stick them to a piece of **unripe fruit** – for instance, a green apple, a plum or a pear.

Leave the fruit in a sunny place to ripen. Remove the paper when the fruit is ripe. Wash off the paste and see your pale initials in the fruit. (You can also initial tomatoes if you like.)

Grass shrieker

There are hundreds of different kinds of grasses. Some are grown by farmers and others grow wild in meadows, ditches, marshland, and even by the seashore.

Try making a shrieking noise with a **blade of grass.** Any kind of grass will do.

Turn the blade so that the edge of the grass is facing toward you.

Hold one end of the grass lengthwise between your thumbs.

Hold the other end of it between the *heels* (or the bottom parts) of your hands.

Your hands should be cupped round the grass and the blade should be stretched tightly.

Now blow across the blade of grass and listen to the shrieking sound you make.

Egging you on

You can make interesting and unusual egg decorations once you know how to hollow out eggs. (Always save the inside of the egg so someone can cook it later.)
Put an **egg** in an **egg-cup.**
1. Gently pierce a hole in one end with a **darning needle.**
Pierce another hole, a little larger, in the other end.
2. Hold the egg over a **bowl** and gently blow into the smaller hole until all the egg comes out at the other end.
Carefully run water through the egg to clean it thoroughly, and then shake it dry.

1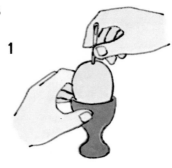

3. Coat half the egg with **PVA glue.**
4. Stick on **braid, wool and tiny beads or seeds.**
Let the glue dry.
Turn the egg and decorate the other half the same way.

2    3   4

Pebble pot

Turn an ordinary flowerpot into a special one.
Look for some **fine gravel or little pebbles.**
1. Coat the outside of the **flowerpot** up to the rim with **strong glue.**
2. Press on pebbles in any pattern you like.
Leave the glue to dry.

1   2

Burr babies

Burrs are the tiny rough seeds of plants such as wild carrot and burdock. They stick to the fur or feathers of animals or birds and they stick to your clothes as well!
In the summer you could collect a paper bag full of **burrs** from fields and meadows.
Try making some models by sticking the burrs to each other.
Use one burr for a doll's head, then stick a lot of burrs together to make a body.
Make animals in the same way.
Or make a shallow burr basket. Stick burrs together to make a bottom. Then shape curved sides out of burrs. If you like, put a small dish of water in the basket and fill it with pretty flowers.

Mind-reading ribbons

This trick should convince your friends that you have some very magical ribbons!

1. Use **small rubber bands** to join **three differently-coloured ribbons** into a circle.

2. Put the ribbon circle into a **paper bag.**

You will need **three more ribbons** the same colours as the ones fastened together.

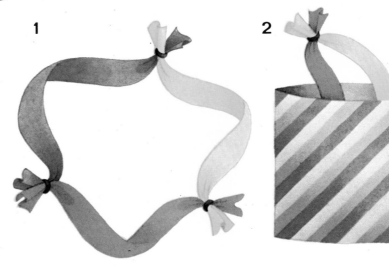

1

2

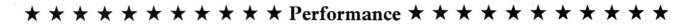
★ ★ ★ ★ ★ ★ ★ ★ ★ ★ ★ ★ **Performance** ★ ★ ★ ★ ★ ★ ★ ★ ★ ★ ★ ★

Give the three spare ribbons to someone in your audience.

3. Ask the person to tie them into a long strip, but not to let you see it.

Show everyone the paper bag. Tell them it holds three ribbons which are able to tie themselves into the same order as the spare strip of ribbons.

4. Ask the person with the spare ribbons to hold up the strip. Look at the colours showing at the top and bottom of the strip. (You must remember what the colours are.)

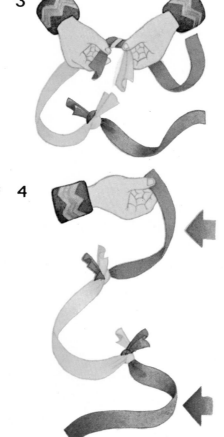

3

4

Dip into the bag and slip off the rubber band that joins the two colours you noticed in the strip.

5. Take hold of the same colour as the other person is holding, and draw the ribbons from the bag.

The order of colours will be the same!

5

Colour jump

This trick works almost by itself.
1. Put a sheet of **red paper** on top of a sheet of **yellow paper**, allowing a 5cm overlap.

1

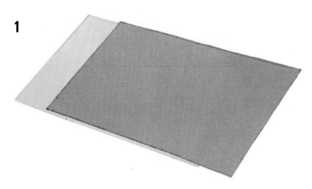

2. Roll the papers up almost to the end of the red sheet of paper.
When you have reached the end of the yellow sheet it will flip right over.

2

3. Now unroll the papers and the yellow one will be on top.

3

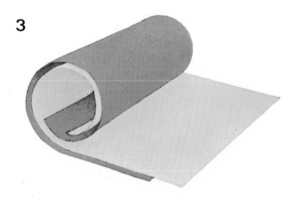

Double six

Here's a way to throw sixes every time.
1. Use **strong glue** to fix **two dice**, sixes up, into one end of a **large matchbox** drawer.

1

2. Drop **two spare dice** into the other end of the drawer and close the box.

2

★★★★ Performance ★★★★

Open the box a little and tip out the loose dice.
Ask someone to drop them back into the box.
3. Shake the box and say you will throw sixes.

3

Keep the box tilted slightly so that the loose dice stay at one end of the drawer.
4. Open the box at the other end to reveal the two glued-down dice with sixes showing.

4

Pecking bird

This little bird will peck for food at the touch of your finger.

Find a **large plain cork**, a **smaller plastic-topped cork** and a **matchbox.**

Paint them all with **poster paint** and a **brush.**

Push **three plastic toothpicks** into the large cork to make the bird's legs and neck. Make sure the toothpicks fit tightly.

Push the plastic-topped cork on to the neck to make the head.

Add **half a toothpick** for the beak and **two map pins** for the eyes.

Find a **feather** for the tail. Make a hole for it with the other piece of toothpick.

Cut out wings from **felt or card** and use **glue** to stick them to the body.

Turn the matchbox upside-down and poke the bird's legs through the box and the drawer.

Push the drawer slightly to and fro, and watch the bird peck away.

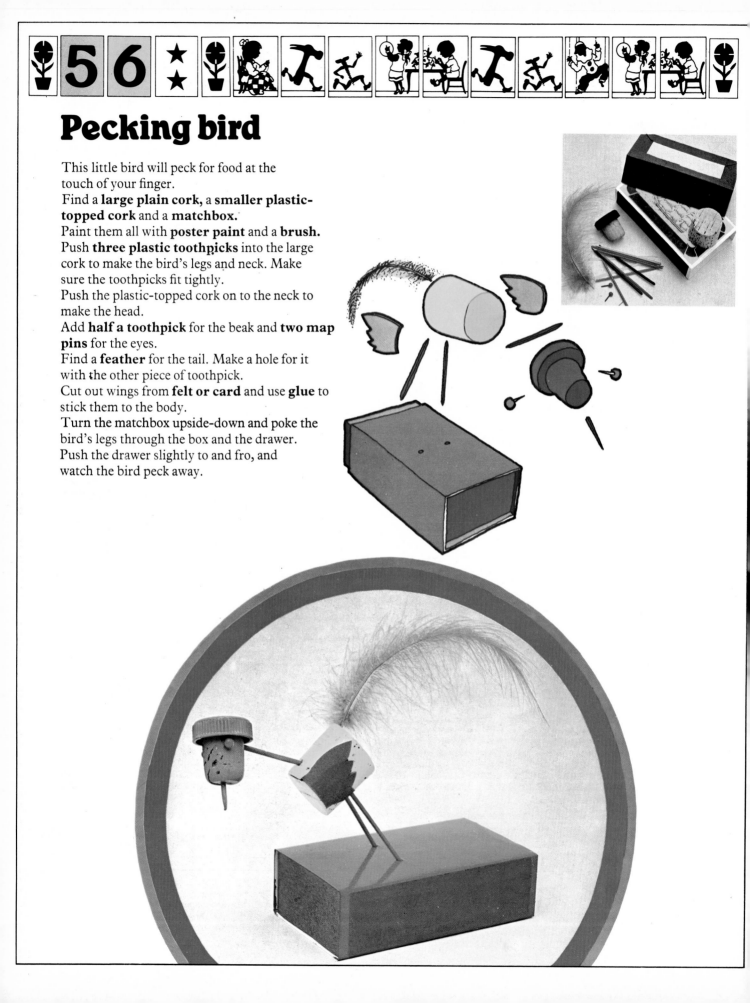

Soup can dragster

Ask an adult to help you make this racing car.
Squash the open end of an **empty soup can.**
Use a **hammer** and **nail** to punch four small
holes in the open end for the front axle.
Punch two larger holes at the other end. Make
the holes big enough to take **6mm dowelling.**
For the wheels, find **two rimmed tin lids** and
two wooden balls with 6mm holes.
Paint them with **acrylic paint** and a **brush.**
Push a piece of dowelling 1cm wider than the
can through the back axle holes.
Fix a piece of dowelling 4cm wider than the can
to the front of the car by threading **wire** through
the holes. Twist the ends of the wire.
With **scissors,** cut a **cardboard** windscreen.
Paint it and the car. Find a **plastic-topped
cork** and paint a face on it for the driver.
Use **strong glue** to stick on the driver, the
windscreen and both sets of wheels.
Add **two corks** for headlamps.

wiggle nail
to make
6mm hole

front
axle
holes

twist ends
of wire

The still coin

Everything has *inertia* (pronounced *in-ersha*). This means that everything needs a force to start it moving. Try this experiment to see that this is true.

1. Put a **small coin** in the middle of a sheet of **cardboard** about 8cm square.
Close your hand to make a fist.
Balance the card on the back of your fist.

2. Keeping your hand perfectly still, flick the card away *very quickly*.

3. The coin will stay on your fist.

1

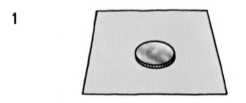

2

3

The coin can only be moved by an external force acting upon it. But when you flick *quickly* at the card, very little of the force in your finger reaches the coin.
If you are in a car that starts suddenly, you feel your body being pressed back against the seat. Your body's inertia acts against the car's movement.

The moving coin

In this experiment you will see how a coin's *momentum* (or motion) keeps it moving.
Prop a piece of **cardboard** up at a slight angle to the floor.
Put a **small coin** on the roof of a **toy car**.

1. Let the car roll down the cardboard slope.

2. When the car stops slowly the coin will remain on the roof.

1   **2**

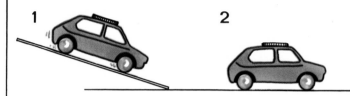

Now put a **thin book** a little way in front of the cardboard slope.

3. Roll the car (with its coin) down the slope.

4. The coin will shoot off the roof when the car stops suddenly against the book.

3   **4**

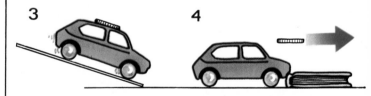

The book stops the car, but its force does not reach the coin so the coin's momentum keeps it moving. In the same way, if you are in a car that stops suddenly, your body's momentum will throw you forward. A seatbelt acts as a force to stop you and keep you safe.

Straight light

Light travels only in straight lines, but it is also reflected from objects. We can see the moon at night because the sun's light travels in a straight line to the moon and the moon reflects it in a straight line to earth. You can easily see for yourself how light travels.

Borrow a **torch** from someone. With **scissors,** cut a piece of **dark-coloured paper** big enough to cover the bulb end of the torch. Fold the paper in half and cut a narrow slit in the middle. Fix the paper over the end of the torch with **sticky tape.**

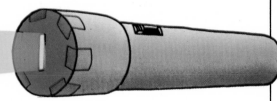

Put out all the lights in a room. Turn the torch on and point it at a **mirror.** The torch beam will be reflected so that it shines on the wall opposite the mirror.

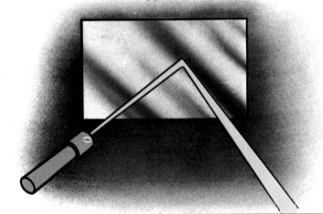

Static balloon

A balloon will remain *static* (or at rest) on a wall if you give it an electrical charge. The amount of electricity is very low and won't hurt you. Blow up a **balloon** and tie the neck tightly. Gently rub the balloon on a piece of **soft clothing** such as a woolly sweater or a pair of nylon stockings.

Now press the balloon carefully against a **wall.** It will stay there for quite some time because the wall, which is uncharged, attracts the charged balloon. As the electrical charge wears down, the attraction is weakened and the balloon will fall off the wall.

Threading ice

This experiment shows that the freezing point of water is lower under pressure.
Put an **ice cube** on a **tray.**
Hold a piece of **strong wire** firmly in both hands and press it down on the ice cube. Press until the wire has gone half-way through. Now you can pick up the ice cube on the wire. The ice cube isn't cut in two because the pressure on the wire melts the ice. Once the wire has passed through, the melted ice re-freezes.

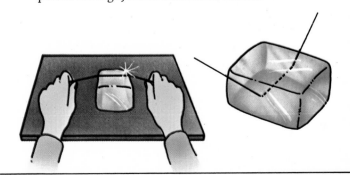

Blow football

Can you imagine a football game played on an ordinary table? This is 'football' with a difference! It is easy to play and a lot of fun.

At each end of a **large table,** arrange some **matchboxes** in a three-sided-box shape to act as the goals.
Put some things along the edge of the table to stop the ball falling off – **more matchboxes or toy building bricks** would do.
The 'football match' can be played either between two players or two teams.

You now need a **ping-pong ball** and **drinking straws** for each of the players.
Decide which goal belongs to each player or team of players.
Put the ball in the centre of the table.
At the word, 'Go!' the players on both sides try to get the ball into their opponents' goal.
(You mustn't touch the ball with your hands.)
Each time a goal is scored the ball is put back in the centre of the table and the game starts again.
The player who scored has first blow.
If a player makes the ball roll off the table, his opponent puts the ball on the spot where it rolled off and re-starts the game.
The player with the most goals at the end of the time (say, ten minutes) is the winner.

Captain's treasure

This is a party game for playing indoors. It's very easy, but **ask an adult** which room you should play in before you start.
You need a **few small objects** as 'treasure' – for instance, a thimble, a stamp, a toothbrush and a coin.

One person is chosen as the 'treasure holder'. All the other players divide into two teams and each team chooses a Captain.
Both teams leave the room while the 'treasure holder' hides the objects in different places.
The teams come in and the 'treasure holder' calls out the name of one of the objects.
Everyone must search for it, but when it is found only the Captain can touch it. He takes it to the 'treasure holder' and his team scores one point.
The 'treasure holder' names another object, and so the game goes on until all the objects have been found.
The team with the most 'treasure' wins.

Jelly shovel

If you like food and sometimes get very hungry, you're sure to enjoy this game.

Put on some **old clothes** and play this game outside because it's a bit messy.
For two players, you will need **two bowls of jelly, two wooden spoons,** and **two blindfolds.**
(**Ask an adult** before you raid the kitchen.)
The players sit opposite each other with their blindfolds on.
Each player holds a bowl of jelly in one hand and a spoon in the other.
They have to feed each other the jelly. The first one with an empty bowl wins.

Score or bust

Here's a good indoor game for a rainy day. You can play it with one or more friends.

'Score or bust' is played with a **dice** which each player throws once when it's his turn. A scorer has a **pencil** and **paper** and writes down the number thrown by each player every time.
The idea is to score a total of 21 or as near to 21 as possible. If anyone scores over 21 he 'busts' and is out of the game.
It doesn't matter how many turns each player has and players can miss a turn if they like.
The first player who scores 21 wins the game.
If no one can get 21, the player with the score closest to it is the winner.

Mapping your diet

Food and wine labels are very attractive. Have you ever noticed the variety of them in the kitchen cupboard? You could start a collection of labels from used tins of food, packets of cheese, bottles of wine, or from fresh fruit.
Soak bottles in **water** to remove their labels. Most labels on tins and boxes can be eased off if you are careful. (**Ask an adult** before you take tins or bottles from the kitchen.)

Labels often tell you where the food or drink came from and collecting them is an interesting way of learning about the world's produce. You could find out all about one or two countries at a time. You might have a label from some Parma ham, for instance, to go on a map of Italy; or from Edam cheese to put on a map of Holland; or from Somerset cider to go on a map of England.
Buy or draw **a map** of a country (or the whole world, if you like) and use **glue** to stick it to a large piece of **cardboard.** Leave room round the edges to add your labels.
With **scissors,** cut lengths of **cotton thread.** Tie the ends of the threads round **map pins.** Put one map pin in the area of the country for which you have a label. (If you have a world map put a pin in a particular country.) Stretch the thread beyond the map and fix the label to the cardboard with the other map pin.

 6 8

A trim picture

Ask an adult if you can collect the **dress trimmings** from any old clothes or from finished sewing projects. Look for lace or crochet on cuffs and collars of blouses, sequins on dresses, ribbons and feathers on hats. You might even find some beautiful beadwork on an old evening dress. Use your prettiest pieces to make unusual cloth pictures or wall hangings.

Cover a piece of **stiff cardboard** with **PVA glue.** Stick down a **plain piece of cloth** on it.

When the glue is dry, use **dressmaker's chalk** to draw a decorative shape on the cloth. You could draw freehand or trace a shape from a magazine. Glue all your trimmings within the outline to make a varied pattern.

---

6 9 ★

Autographs

If you are interested in famous footballers, pop stars or authors you could make a hobby of collecting their *autographs* (or signatures).

You could write to a famous person asking for an autograph. If you don't know his or her address, write 'care of' the sports ground, theatre, recording or film company where the person works and enclose a stamped, self-addressed envelope. If you write an interesting letter you may get a signed photograph or programme or even a letter in return.

Keep an **autograph book** so that you can paste in your signatures with **glue.** You might be lucky enough to see a famous person in the street or in a restaurant, so carry your book and a **pen** with you when you go out.

Free your friend

Imagine that someone has imprisoned your best friend inside this castle. The castle is surrounded by a moat 3 metres wide.

You've come to rescue your friend but the two planks you have brought with you are only 2.97 metres long. Both planks are 3 centimetres too short and you have no way of fixing them together.

How can you arrange the two planks so that you are able to cross the moat ?

(The answer is in the back of the book.)

Fishy problem

One of these fish is swimming in the wrong part of its sea circle. Can you see where it should be ?

(The answer is in the back of the book.)

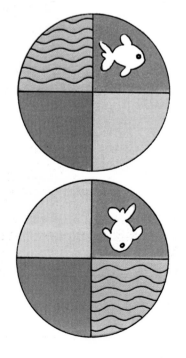

Mouse maze

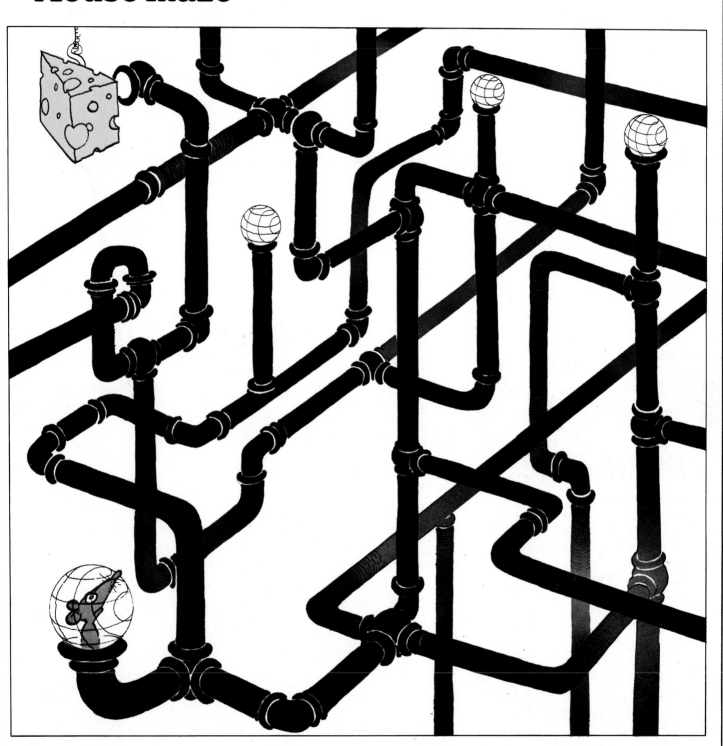

This little mouse can see a tasty lump of cheese but he has to find his way through the pipes to get it. Can you help him?

Trace your path with your finger or put **tracing paper** over the page and use a **pencil.**
(You'll find the route in the back of the book.)

Water pistols

Have fun out of doors with these pistols, but be sure to put on old clothes first.

Pull the squirter nozzles off **two empty washing-up liquid bottles.** Wash the bottles inside and out. Leave them to dry.

1. Paint the bottles with **acrylic paints** and a **paintbrush.** Let the colours dry.

2. Fill the bottles with **water,** and replace the squirter nozzles.

Stand back-to-back with a friend, each of you holding a bottle pistol in both hands. Slowly walk three paces forward, turn and . . . squeeze!

Nailophone

Ask an adult to help you make an unusual musical instrument that plays in the breeze.

Buy a metre of **heavy galvanised wire** and **eight 8cm-long nails** from a hardware shop. From a plant shop or garden centre buy a metre-long **bamboo or cane rod.**

1. Bend the wire into a snaky shape.

2. Tie a 35cm length of **string** to each end of the wire and hang it from the rod.

Use **scissors** to cut eight pieces of **strong cotton,** each 40cm long.

3. Tie one length of cotton to each nail.

4. Hang the nails in a row along the rod so that their tips come just below the wire.

Use **more string** to tie the nailophone to a **tree branch or a window curtain rail.** When the wind blows, the nails will 'ping' against the wire.

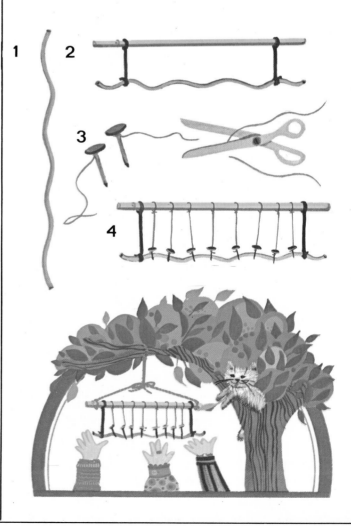

Party place mats

Colourful mats make a party table look festive. Make some from **differently-coloured papers.** With a **ruler** and **pencil,** measure and mark ten strips of paper each 30cm by 3cm.

1. Use **scissors** to cut out the strips.

In the same way, measure and cut eight more strips of paper, each 36cm by 3cm.

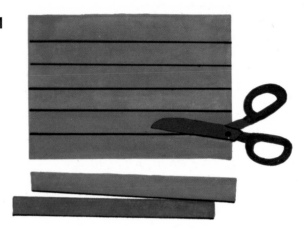

Put the ten short strips side by side on a table. Arrange the colours any way you like.

2. Starting half-way down the ten strips, weave the eight longer strips in and out between the shorter ones.

Leave about 3cm at each edge of the mat.

start weaving here and work outwards

fold over and glue

3. Fold over the ends all round the mat and stick them down with **glue.**

Make more mats in the same way.

Warming up

You need a few people in your audience to be able to do this magical trick.
Put several **coins** in a **box**.
Tell your audience that you can pick out a coin someone else chooses without seeing it first.
Ask someone to take out any coin while your back is turned.
Ask for the coin to be passed round so that everyone can look at it and remember it.
Then the coin must be put back in the box.
When you turn round, feel about in the box for the warmest coin and take it out.
Everyone will be amazed when they see that it is the right one.

Vanishing number

This is a very cunning trick.
Tell your audience that you can make a number disappear from a sheet of paper.
Use a **pencil** to write the numbers between one and nine in a straight line along the top of a sheet of **paper.**
Ask someone to call out any number.
Fold up the bottom corner of the paper so that it covers the chosen number but leaves the other numbers visible.
Your audience will realise that it's a trick, but you have done what you said you could do!

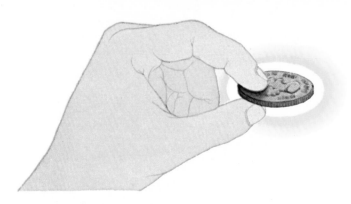

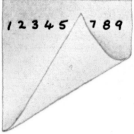

Adding master

Practise adding in your head, then copy these numbers in **pencil** on to five pieces of **card**.

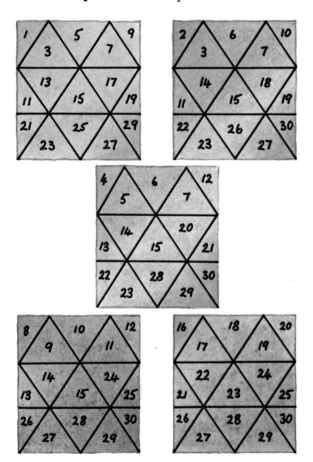

★★★★ **Performance** ★★★★

Give all the cards to someone and say you can name any number he or she secretly chooses simply by looking at the cards.

Ask the person to think of any number between one and 30 and to give you back all the cards that bear the chosen number.

In your head, add up the numbers in the *top left-hand corner* of each of the cards that have been handed to you.

Your total will be the chosen number.

X-ray eyes

Make believe that you have X-ray vision!
Cut two small **cardboard** circles with **scissors**.
1. Fix a **hair** to one with **sticky tape,** then use **glue** to stick the cardboard circles together.
2. Cut three cardboard shapes as shown. Fold into pointed hats and tape the joins together.

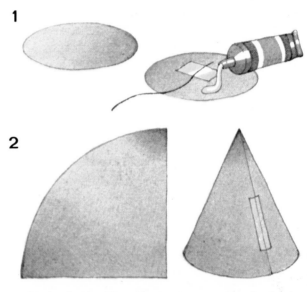

★★★★ **Performance** ★★★★

Ask someone to cover the circle with one hat while your back is turned.
When you turn round, look for the hair sticking out from under one of the hats.
Then you can say which hat hides the circle.

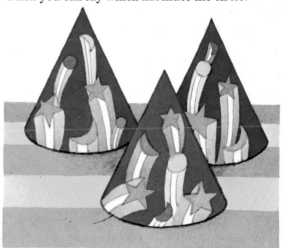

How time flies

Here's a way to make a **watch (or any small object)** disappear.
Use **glue** to stick the top of a **small paper bag** to the inside top of a **big paper bag**.

★★★ Performance ★★★★

Show your audience the watch and say you can make it disappear.
1. Put the watch in the small paper bag.
(Everyone will think it is in the big bag.)
2. Blow up the big bag and burst it.
3. Show the empty torn bag. (The watch is still hidden in the small paper bag, but it will seem to have disappeared.)

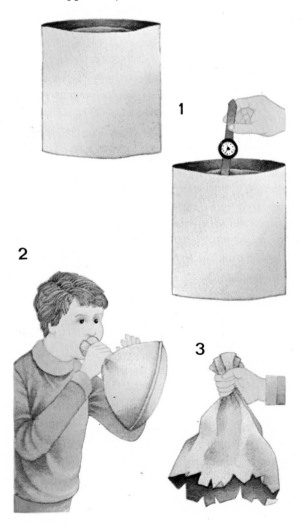

Turning point

This very easy trick works almost by itself.
Use a **felt-tipped pen** to draw an arrow on a small piece of **cardboard**.
Put the cardboard behind a **glass tumbler**.
Ask someone to look through the tumbler as you pour **water** into it.
When the tumbler is almost full the arrow will seem to turn and point in the other direction.

Great divide

Cut a strip of paper, yet leave it whole!
Cut two equal strips of **paper** with **scissors**.
1. Use **glue** to stick both pieces together, leaving a small unglued gap in the middle.
2. Fold one strip downward into a point at the middle, then fold the paper in half.

★★★ Performance ★★★★

3. Hold the paper in your hand and cut right across the unglued fold.
Open out the strip and it will still be whole.

Big attraction

This trick makes your hand look magnetic.
Find a few **old playing cards.**
1. With **scissors,** cut a small square from one of the cards.
2. Fold the square in half and use **glue** to stick half of it to the back of another card.

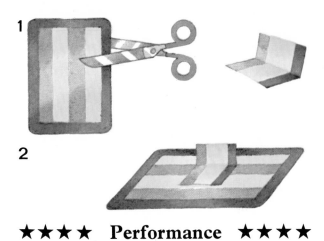

★★★★ **Performance** ★★★★

3. Put the special card, picture side facing upward, on the palm of your hand.
(You will find that you can hold the unglued part of the secret square between your fingers. Don't let anyone see the secret square.)
Use your other hand to slide more cards between the special card and your palm.
4. Carefully turn your palm over.
All the cards will seem to be sticking to your hand, just as nails stick to a magnet.

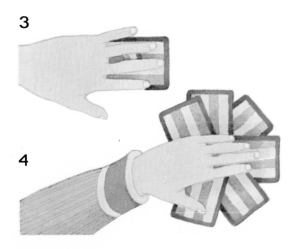

Shell garden

When you go to the seaside look among the rocks for **whelk or scallop shells.** Make sure there are no creatures living inside them.
At home, wash the shells in **hot, soapy water.**
Use **tweezers** to pick out any bits left inside.
Rinse the shells in **clean water** and leave them on a **newspaper** to dry.
(If you like, you could varnish the outside of the shells with polyurethane varnish and a brush to make them shiny.)
Mount the shell in a small lump of **plasticine** so that it sits flat.
Fill the shell with **soil.**
Plant some **mustard and cress or miniature ivy** in the shell.

Pied flower

Choose a **white flower** such as a chrysanthemum or carnation and change its colour.
Slit the stem half-way up with a **kitchen knife.**
Put the two halves in **two glass tumblers.**
Put **water** in one tumbler.
In the other, put two teaspoons of **glycerine** and some **coloured ink or food dye.**
Watch the flower change colour as it draws the dye up its stem.

Pot-pourri

A *pot-pourri* is a mixture of dried flower petals, leaves and spices. Gather lots of **flower petals** and **leaves** to make a pretty, perfumed mixture for your room. Choose scented flowers such as roses, jasmine, violets, primulas and jonquils. Pick rose leaves and the leaves of basil, lavender, sage, marjoram or thyme. From a herbalist or chemist buy a tiny packet of **orris-root powder** – this will help to preserve the colour and scent of a pot-pourri for a long time.

1. Put the petals and leaves on **paper** in a dry, airy place out of direct sunlight. Turn them often until they are completely dry. Mix petals and leaves in a **bowl.** Try to get a good balance of colour as well as the perfume you like best.

2. Add one **teaspoon** of orris-root to every half-litre of mixture. Add the same amount of **spices** – cloves, allspice, or nutmeg for instance. Add a few drops of flower oils (from a herbalist) if you like. Stir the mixture with a **spoon.**

3. Put the mixture in a **screw-top jar** and store it for six weeks. When it is ready, open the jar for a little while each day. Or tip the mixture into a bowl. The pot-pourri will lose its perfume more quickly, but it looks especially pretty this way.

Japanese lake

The Japanese regard ornamental gardens and lakes as works of art – just like beautiful paintings or fine poetry. The secret in making a miniature Japanese lake is not to clutter it with too many different things.

You will need a **shallow glass dish or bowl.**

1. Line the bottom with 2.5cm of ordinary **soil** and cover it with a layer of **gravel.**
2. Push a tiny piece of **driftwood or dried twigs** into the soil and gravel.

Buy two or three **miniature water-lilies** from a florist or plant shop.

Plant the lilies in the soil and gravel.

3. Pour enough **water** into the bowl to just cover the lilies.

Keep adding water as the lilies grow.

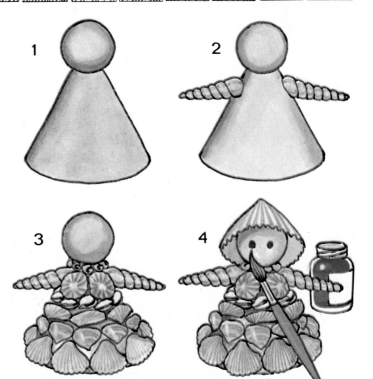

Shell lady

Next time you go to the seaside, collect some **small shells.** When you get home, wash off the sand and use the shells to make a model.

First, shape a body out of **self-hardening clay.** Roll a smooth ball of clay about the size of a ping-pong ball for the head. Make a cone shape for the body.

1. Moisten the top of the triangle with **water** and press the ball on to it.
2. To make arms, press in pointed tower or needle shells.
3. Decorate the skirt with cowries, cockles, thin tellin, carpet or banded wedge shells.

Use a limpet shell for a hat.

4. With **poster paints** and a **brush,** paint on a nose, mouth and eyes.

Seven-up

You can play this ball game on your own or with other players. It's called 'Seven-up' because you have to catch a **ball** seven different ways in a certain order. You can make up the ways and their order yourself if you like, but here is a set of ways to start with:

1. Throw the ball against a **wall** and clap your hands once before catching it.
2. Throw the ball against a wall and clap twice before catching it.
3. Throw the ball against a wall and clap your hands over your head before catching it.
4. Throw the ball against a wall and spin round once before catching it.
5. Throw the ball against a wall and let it bounce under one leg before catching it.
6. Throw the ball against a wall and touch the ground before catching it.
7. Throw the ball against a wall and let it bounce on your head before catching it.

Hot bricks

Persuade everyone to join in this musical game next time you have a party. You'll soon see that music and parties go very well together.

You will need **records** and a **record player or a radio** and a **small object** such as a bean bag or a soft toy. This is called the 'hot brick'.
All the players sit in a circle except one person who is in charge of the music.
When the music starts the 'hot brick' is passed round the circle. When the music stops the player holding the 'brick' must drop out.
The game goes on until there is a winner – only one person who has not held the 'hot brick'.

Deep freeze

Play this game indoors or outside with either a few or lots of players.
Mark a starting line about 6 or 8 metres from a **wall (or a tree).**
Choose one player to be 'It'.
All the other players stand behind the starting line and 'It' faces the wall.
The others have to try to creep up and touch 'It' without being caught moving. If 'It' turns round everyone must stop moving, or freeze on the spot.
Anyone caught moving must go back to the start.
The player who manages to touch 'It' then faces the wall and play starts again.

Blind man's buff

Older children will probably know this game well but here it is again for their younger brothers, sisters and friends to learn.

One player puts on a **blindfold.**

All the others dance round in a circle until the 'blind person' commands them to stop.

The blindfolded player points a finger and the player pointed to must come forward.

The 'blind person' has to try to guess who it is by touch or by asking any question except, 'Who are you ?'.

If he or she guesses correctly the player who has been caught is blindfolded.

Otherwise the game continues until the 'blind person' is able to identify someone.

Round the clock

The idea of this game is to throw all the numbers (one to 12) on a clock face using a **dice.**

Someone with a **pencil** and **paper** keeps score.

Taking it in turns, each player throws the dice for one, then two, and so on up to six.

When a player has thrown a six he tries for one again to make up seven, then for two to make eight, and so on until he makes 12.

The first to throw 'round the clock' wins.

Cops and robbers

When it's cold or wet outside ask a friend or someone in the family to play this indoor 'hunting' game with you. All you need is an ordinary **draught board** and some **draughts.**

Put four black draughts on the black squares at one end of the board. These are the 'cops'.

Put one white draught on a white square at the other end of the board. This is the 'robber'.

The 'robber' has to try to reach the opposite end of the board. The 'cops' have to try to box him in so that he cannot move. (There is no jumping over draughts in this game.)

The first move is made by one of the 'cops'.

A 'cop' can only move one space at a time, and only in one direction – forward.

The 'robber' can move one space at a time in *any* direction, but only on the white squares.

Reeling tank

This 'tank' is powered by energy stored in a rubber band. (This is called *potential* energy.) Wind up the band and see what happens.

1. Use a **short pencil** to push a **rubber band** through an **empty cotton reel.**

1

2. Hook one end of the rubber band over a **paper clip** and fix the clip to the cotton reel with **sticky tape.**

2

3. Loop the other end of the rubber band over the pencil. This makes the 'tank'.

3

4. Turn the pencil round and round until the rubber band is twisted tightly.

4

Still holding the cotton reel and pencil, put the 'tank' on the floor. When you let go, the 'tank' will race round the room.

Magnifying lens

When something is *magnified* it looks bigger. Water will act as a magnifier. Make this water-drop magnifying lens and see for yourself.

1. With a **pencil,** draw this shape on **stiff cardboard** 18cm by 9cm. Cut round the lines with **scissors.**

1

2

Cut a piece of **plastic** to fit the circular part.
2. Stretch the plastic over the hole and fix it with **sticky tape.**

3. Put a **drop of water** on the plastic. Hold the lens over this page to magnify the words.

3

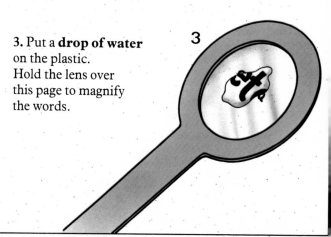

Light fader

Salty water is a conductor for the electricity that makes this toy work. The light fader can't possibly hurt you, but **ask an adult** to help because there are many steps to follow. Use the light in a toy theatre or dolls' house.

From an electrical shop buy: one **4½ volt battery,** one **3½ volt bulb, a bulb holder,** and 1.60 metres of **thin electrical wire.**
Use **scissors** to cut the wire into two 30cm-long pieces and one 1 metre-long piece.
1. Cut and strip off 2cm of plastic covering from each end of all three pieces of wire.

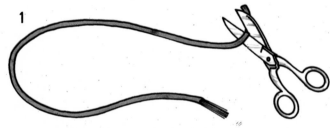

2. Fix one short length of wire to each contact on the battery.
Screw the bulb into the bulb holder.

3. Fix the other end of one wire to one screw of the bulb holder.

4. Fix the long piece of wire to the other screw of the bulb holder.

Now make *terminals* (the ends of the electrical circuit). You will need two pieces of **silver paper, two paper clips** and **sticky tape.**
5. Tape an opened-out paper clip to the two spare ends of wire.
6. Fold a piece of silver paper round each paper clip and bend the spare paper up.
Fill a **glass** with **water.** Add **salt,** stirring with a **spoon,** until no more salt will dissolve.

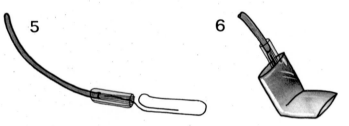

7. Bend the wire so that one silver paper terminal sits at the bottom of the glass.

8. Put the other terminal into the water.
You'll see the bulb get brighter as the terminals come closer together.

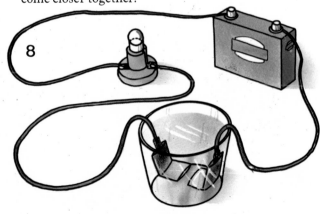

Peg doll

With a little patience you can turn an old-fashioned clothes-peg into a pretty doll.

With a **ruler,** measure the height of a **wooden clothes-peg.**
Use **scissors** to cut out a square of **cloth** to the same measurement.

1. With a **needle** and **cotton thread,** run a gathering stitch along the top of the cloth. Use **glue** to join the centre back seam. Gather the cloth and tie it round the peg.

3. Paint a face on the doll with **acrylic paints** and a **brush.**

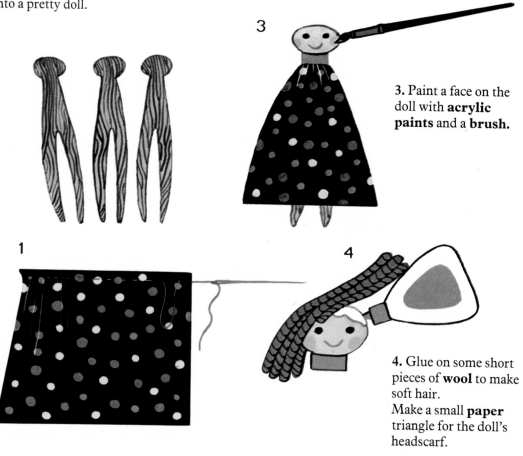

4. Glue on some short pieces of **wool** to make soft hair.
Make a small **paper** triangle for the doll's headscarf.

2. Glue a piece of **ribbon** round the neck.

Make an impression

'How you've grown!' your mother will say when she sees a plaster print of your hand.

1

Mix **plaster of Paris** with **water** until it is smooth and stiff. Pour the plaster into a **foil pie dish.**

1. Press your hand into the plaster. Keep your hand still until you feel the plaster begin to set. Ask a friend to make a hand print, too, to keep you company.

2. Remove your hand gently when you can take it away without taking plaster too.

Scratch your initials into the plaster with the wrong end of a **paintbrush.**

2

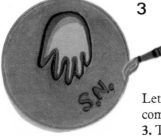

3

Let the plaster dry completely.
3. Turn the plaster out of the dish and paint it with **acrylic or poster paint.**

Wax rubbings

You'll really begin to notice different designs if you take wax rubbings of things. A rubbing can be taken from anything which has an uneven surface. Find things round the house – wooden mouldings, fire grates, keyhole surrounds, raised printing or designs on window glass and books, or textured wallpaper. Then have a look in your neighbourhood for coal-hole covers, water-hydrant lids, interesting bark on trees or brickwork on buildings.

Use a **cloth** to dust the **uneven surface** you want to rub.
1. Put a sheet of **white paper** over it.
Fix the paper down with **masking tape.**

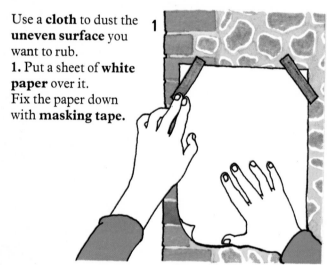

2. Rub slowly and carefully to and fro with a **wax crayon.** Make sure you rub in one direction only. You will soon see the pattern transferring itself to the paper.

If you make a hobby of collecting different wax rubbings you may like to mount them in frames. To make a frame, cut a rectangle out of **stiff white or coloured cardboard.**
1. Fold the rectangle in half.
2. Use **scissors** to cut a window in one side. (You could decorate the cardboard by painting it or by gluing on bits of lace.)
Trim your wax rubbing so that it is a little bigger than the window in the frame.
Use **glue** to stick the rubbing in position behind the window.
If you have sheets of rubbings left over you could use them as wrapping paper for presents.

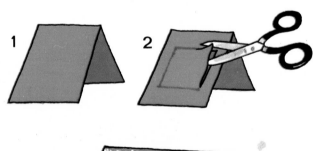

Bottle museum

You might see bottles in a real museum because some old ones are very valuable. Many modern **bottles** are also worth collecting for their beautiful shapes or for the unusual lettering pressed into the glass.

Ask your family and friends to save for you their empty scent bottles, wine or liqueur bottles and old medicine jars.

Look for old bottles yourself in the shed or garage or on land where people throw their rubbish. Watch out for bottles with decorations such as crests or seals impressed on them, for bottles with unusual necks or for ones made of coloured glass. Most bottles you find will probably be very dirty so soak them in **warm, soapy water** to clean them. Rinse the bottles in **clean water** and leave them on **newspaper** to dry.

Make a **card** label for each bottle in your own museum. Use a **pen** to write in the date and place it was found or who gave it to you.
Fill up your bottles with coloured stones or coloured water, if you like.

Nail design

Nails differ in shape, size and colour. Some have big heads, others have no heads at all; some nails are long and thick and others are tiny; some are steel-grey and a few are a golden copper colour. See how many different kinds of **nails** you can find. Hunt for old nails in the garage and round the house. Or buy some new ones from a hardware or do-it-yourself shop.
Ask an adult to help you display nails on a piece of **softwood.**

1. Use a **thick pencil** to draw an interesting design on the wood.

Work out where each nail goes in the wood.
2. Drive in the nails with a **hammer,** following the lines of the design.

3. For variation, you could use **strong glue** to fix some of the nails flat against the wood.

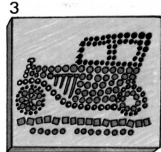

Cunning kitty

The order of events has been mixed up in this series of pictures. Can you sort it out? The top left-hand scene is the first in the series.
(The order is shown in the back of the book.)

Ends to ends

How many bottles can you find in this picture?
(The answer is given in the back of the book.)

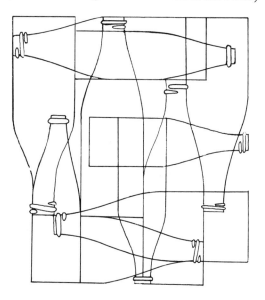

Load of problems

A man is driving a big transport lorry along a country road. He feels cheerful because he is on schedule. Suddenly he comes to a railway bridge bearing a sign which reads: 'Low bridge. Clearance 4 metres.'
The driver stops in a hurry because he knows his lorry is exactly 4.025 metres high!
He gets out and thinks about the problem. The crates of goods are too heavy to lift off the lorry and he doesn't want to take an alternative route because he will lose time. Eventually he works out a way to get the lorry under the bridge. What does the driver do?
(The answer is given in the back of the book.)

Among the stars

This coloured star is made up of five pieces. Can you find another star made up of only four?
Here's a clue: try holding the book away from you. (You can see where the star is in the back of the book.)

After-dinner gardens

The pips, seeds and stones from fresh raw fruit can be grown into new plants if you sow them in the spring. Try growing a lovely tree from an avocado stone. Then you could grow other plants from their seeds.

Avocado tree
Wash the **avocado stone** in water to clean it. Leave it to dry.
1. Push **four toothpicks** into the stone about a third of the way up from the rounded end.

2. Rest the stone in a **jar** filled with **warm water** so that the round end sits in the liquid.
Leave the jar in a warm, dimly-lit place until the stone sprouts, or produces some roots.

3. Put some pebbles in the bottom of a **10cm-deep flowerpot** and then fill the pot with **damp potting soil.**
4. Plant the avocado stone in the soil and leave it in a sunny place.
(Don't forget to water the avocado plant when the soil feels dry.)

A green display
Make the kitchen window-sill bright with other plants grown from seeds.
All **seeds** should be cleaned and dried first.
Don't forget to put **pebbles** in the **flowerpots** before adding **damp potting soil.**
Plant **one or two seeds** of a lemon or orange 2 or 3cm deep.
Plant just one seed in each pot for cherry, peach, plum, marrow or melon plants.
To grow tomatoes or peppers, plant two or three seeds to a pot. Then cover the pot with **glass** until the plants begin to sprout.
Make sure all your plants sit in a sunny spot.

Natural dyes

Dye your own T-shirts with colours you have made yourself. **Ask an adult** to help you because the dye has to be boiled up on a stove.

Here is a list of colours and the natural things that can produce them:

Pink or red
Beetroot; blackberries

Blue
Cornflowers; hollyhocks

Orange or tan
Onion skins; tea leaves

Yellow
Marigold petals; peach leaves

Green
Nettles; spinach

Brown
Walnut shells

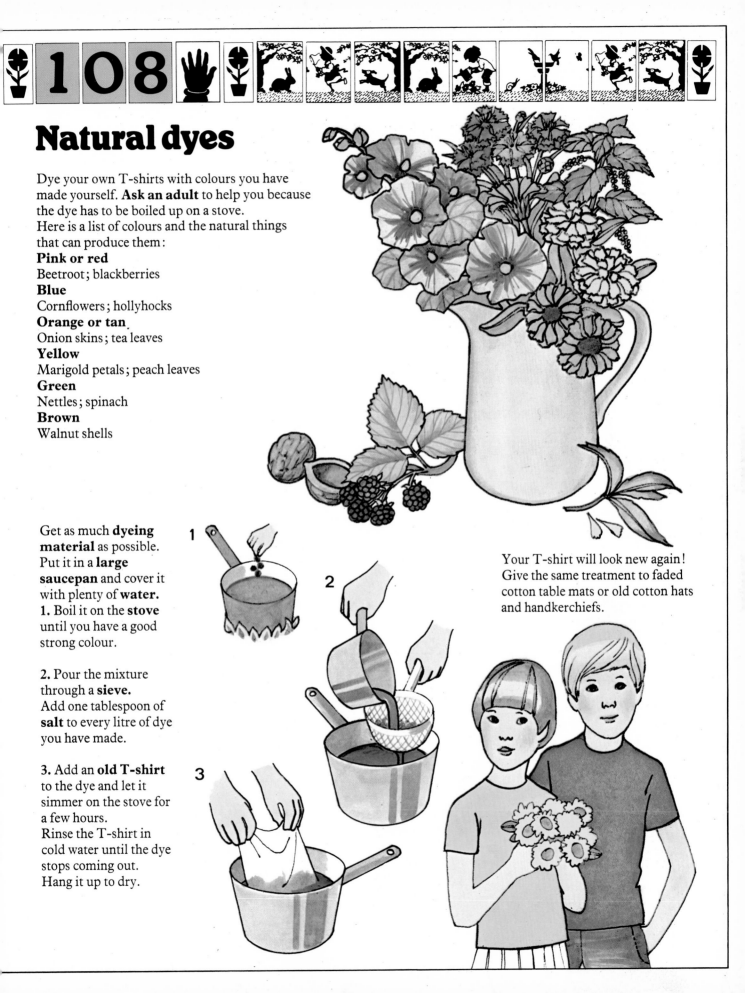

Get as much **dyeing material** as possible. Put it in a **large saucepan** and cover it with plenty of **water**.
1. Boil it on the **stove** until you have a good strong colour.

2. Pour the mixture through a **sieve**. Add one tablespoon of **salt** to every litre of dye you have made.

3. Add an **old T-shirt** to the dye and let it simmer on the stove for a few hours. Rinse the T-shirt in cold water until the dye stops coming out. Hang it up to dry.

Your T-shirt will look new again! Give the same treatment to faded cotton table mats or old cotton hats and handkerchiefs.

Flower power

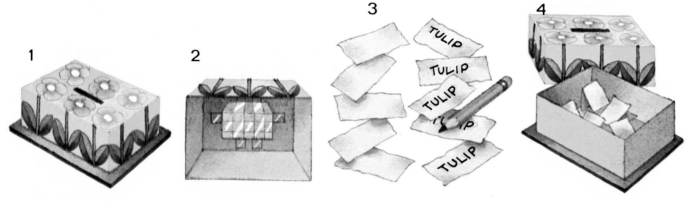

1 **2** **3** **4**

Prepare this special box and astonish your audience with your 'guessing' ability.
1. Use **scissors** to cut a slot in the lid of a **big chocolate box.**
2. With **sticky tape,** fix a **small open-topped box** under the slot of the big lid.

3. Cut twice as many small slips of **paper** as you will have spectators in your audience.
On half the slips write 'tulip' in pencil.
4. Fold the slips in half and drop them into the bottom of the big chocolate box.
Put the lid on the box.

★ ★ ★ ★ ★ ★ ★ ★ ★ ★ Performance ★ ★ ★ ★ ★ ★ ★ ★ ★ ★

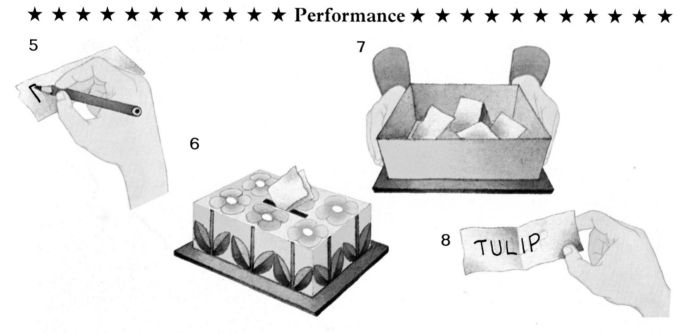

5 **6** **7** **8 TULIP**

Tell everyone you can guess accurately.
Give out **pencils** and the blank slips of paper.
5. Ask your spectators to write the name of any flower on their slips of paper.
6. Then ask for the papers to be folded and put into the box through the slit in the lid.

Shake the box, and then remove the lid.
7. Ask someone to take out any slip.
8. You are able to tell the audience that the name of the flower on the slip is 'tulip'.
(Don't let anyone see the little box under the big lid – that's where the other slips are!)

Wash-off picture

This method of painting makes a picture seem to come from nowhere! Lightly draw a design in **pencil** on a sheet of **rough-textured white paper.**
Fix it to a **window** with **masking tape** and fill in the drawing with **white poster paint** and a **brush.** Remove the picture from the window and leave it to dry.

Paint over the whole sheet with **waterproof black Indian ink.** Let the ink dry completely.
Run **cold water** over the paper and rub the painting gently with your finger. As the ink washes off the parts you painted, an unusual picture will appear.

Snowball

Have snow all year round! To make the snowball, first **ask an adult** for a **white plastic bag.** Remember *never* put a plastic bag over your head and *never* let a baby play with one.

1. Use **scissors** to cut up part of the plastic bag into tiny snippets.
2. Put the snippets into a **screw-top jar** and fill it almost to the top with **water.**

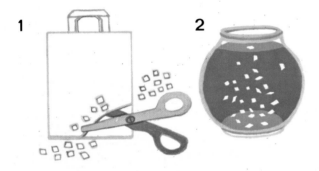

3. Use **glue** to stick a **small plastic toy** to the underside of the lid. Let the glue dry.
Screw the lid tightly to the jar and turn the snowball upside down to make the 'snow' fall.

Non-stop twirler

Hang this snaky twirler in your bedroom and it will keep moving while you're fast asleep.
1. Use a **pencil** to draw round a **small plate** on **thin cardboard.**
2. Cut out the circle and make a small hole in the centre with the point of the **scissors.**
Working outward from the middle, draw a spiral on the cardboard as shown.
3. Cut along the spiral from the edge of the cardboard to the centre.
Tie a knot in one end of a piece of **string.**
4. Thread the string through the centre hole.
Fix the other end of the string to the ceiling with **masking tape.** If you hang the twirler over a radiator the heat will make it turn. *Do not hang it over any other kind of heat or fire.*

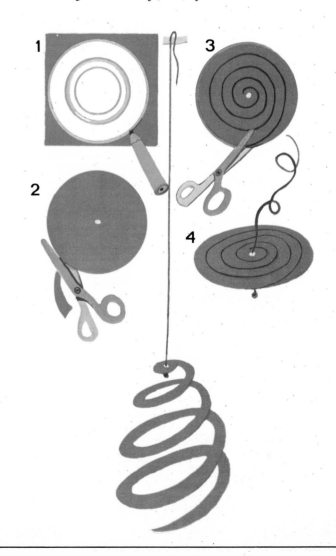

Paper doll chains

Chains of dolls make pretty decorations.
1. Bend a strip of **paper** into zigzag pleats as shown. Fold all the pleats together.

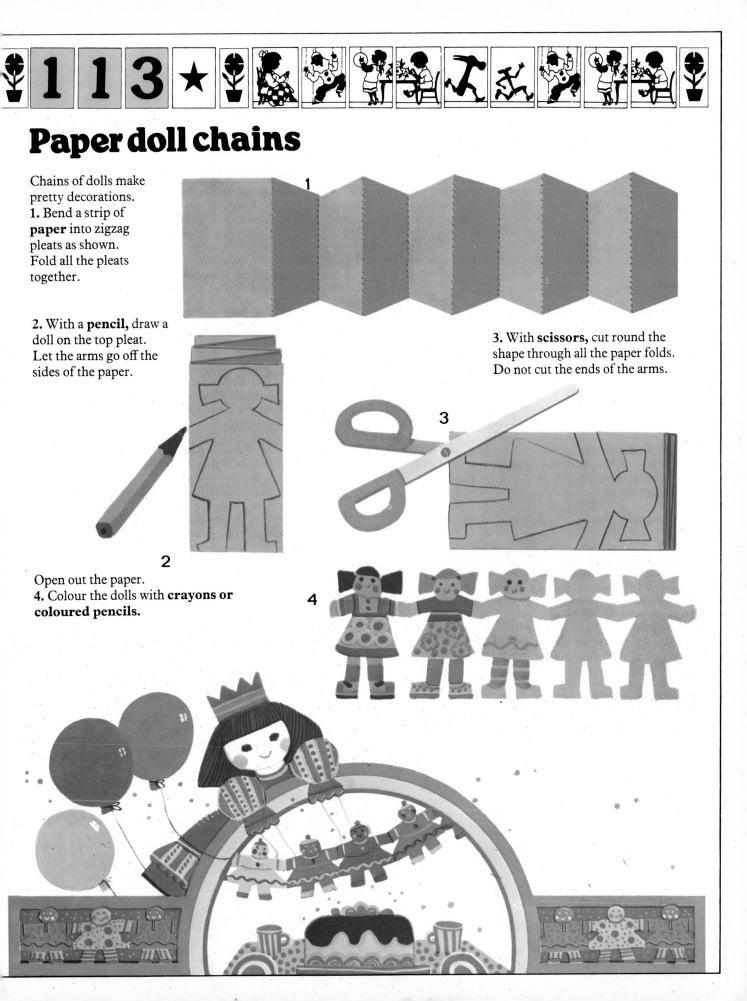

1

2. With a **pencil,** draw a doll on the top pleat. Let the arms go off the sides of the paper.

2

3. With **scissors,** cut round the shape through all the paper folds. Do not cut the ends of the arms.

3

Open out the paper.
4. Colour the dolls with **crayons or coloured pencils.**

4

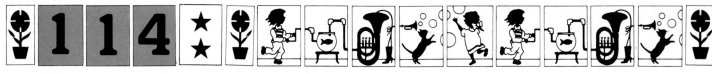
Boomerang drum

As this drum moves away from you, the rubber band inside it stores up the energy needed to drive it back again.

1. Roll up a strip of **stiff paper** 100cm by 15cm into a cylinder about 10cm in diameter.
Fix the join with **sticky tape.**
Stand the cylinder on a piece of **stiff cardboard** about 30cm by 15cm.
2. Draw round the cylinder with a **pencil.**
Use **scissors** to cut out the circle.
Cut another circle in the same way.

3. Tape one of **four paper clips** to an **8cm-long rubber band** as shown.
Hook another paper clip through the one fixed to the rubber band.
4. Mould a lump of **plasticine** round it.
With the point of the scissors, make a small hole in the middle of each cardboard circle.

5. Push one end of the rubber band through the hole in one cardboard circle.
6. Thread a paper clip through the end of the rubber band and tape it to the circle.
7. Tape the circle to the end of the cylinder.
Pull the spare end of the rubber band through the cylinder.

8. Push it through the hole in the other circle and tape it to the cardboard.
Position the circle on the end of the cylinder and tape it into place.
Decorate the drum with **coloured pencils or felt-tipped pens** if you like.

Put the drum on the floor and roll it away from you. When it stops it will begin to roll back towards you.
You can 'wind up' your drum so that it rolls along by itself if you turn it round and round in your hands for a few seconds.

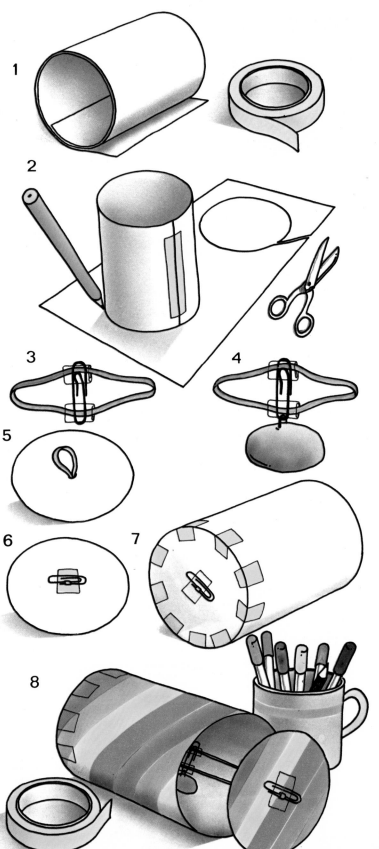

Sugar wall

Try a little experiment to see how a damp-proof course functions in the brickwork of a house.
Ask an adult if you can have some **sugar lumps** and some **cold coffee or tea.**
Build a wall of sugar lumps in a **shallow dish.**
Cut a piece of **plastic** big enough to cover the top row of the wall.
Build another wall of sugar lumps in the dish, putting the piece of plastic between the first and second rows of sugar lumps.
Pour a little cold coffee or tea into the dish.
The first wall you built will soak up the liquid and turn completely brown.
The second wall will be protected above its layer of damp-proof plastic and only the bottom row will soak up the liquid.

Floating egg

Ask your friends if they can make an egg float in water.
Usually, when anyone puts an egg in water it sinks.
Now show them how to make it float.
Add **salt** to a **glass of water** and stir it with a **spoon** until no more salt will dissolve.
Gently put the **egg** in the salty water and it will float!

The egg floats because salty water is heavier than tap water.
A heavy liquid supports more weight than a light one.
For the same reason, a swimmer floats more easily in the salty sea than in fresh water.

Spot the ring

Here is a party game that can be played by very young children as well as older ones.

You will need **several metres of string** and a **curtain ring.** Tie the ends of the string to the ring so that it makes a huge loop.

Everyone sits in a circle except one player who stands in the middle. He is the guesser.

When the guesser says 'Go!' the other players run the string through their hands so that the ring moves round the circle.

When the guesser calls 'Stop!' everyone closes their hands over the string. The guesser then has two guesses to find out who has the ring.

If the guesser is right the player holding the ring goes into the middle. If the guesser is wrong he is out and sits down in the middle.

The other players then choose another guesser.

Pea race

This is a game for an even number of players. You will need as many **saucers** and **drinking straws** as there are players, and a packet of **dried peas.** Here is how four people play:
Put two saucers with ten peas in each of them on one side of the room. Two players stand beside these saucers.

Each player has a partner who stands near an empty saucer on the opposite side of the room. All the players have a drinking straw. The first players have to get their ten peas into their partners' saucers by sucking one pea at a time on to the end of the straws and carrying it across the room.

The partners have to bring all ten peas back. The first pair to finish wins the game.

French cricket

This is a game for a sunny day.
Mark a small circle on the ground
with **chalk or a stick.**
A batsman, holding a **cricket bat
or plank of wood,** stands inside
the circle.
The other players form a ring about
2 metres away from him.
One of the players has a **rubber
ball or tennis ball.**

The ball must be rolled along the
ground or bounced at the batsman,
who has to try and strike it away with
his bat.
The batsman must not move his feet
at all.
The ball can be passed back and
forth among the other players.
They must try to hit the batsman's
legs below the knees with it.

The batsman needs to be very alert
in this game. The ball can be thrown
at the back of his legs where it is
difficult to fend off. By hitting the
ball a long way the batsman can give
himself some breathing space.
When someone hits the batsman or
makes him lose balance, that player
takes his turn with the bat.

Fine and feathery

Birds' feathers are incredibly varied and once you have looked at a few you will begin to see how lovely they are. When you are in the country or by the seaside watch out for the feathers of wild birds. Look in library books about birds to identify the feathers you find. Or visit the poulterer and ask for duck, goose, chicken or turkey feathers for your collection.

If you have just a few feathers, why not make a feather duster for your mother or for an aunt?

Feather duster

Simply use **sticky tape** to bind the **feathers** to a **bamboo or cane rod** about 30cm long.

Feather choker

Show off your most beautiful feathers by combining them with ribbon and **beads**.

Slip a bead on each end of some **short pieces of ribbon or cord.** Knot the ends.

1

1. Using a **needle** and **cotton thread,** sew one feather to the middle of each length of ribbon or cord.

2

2. Tie the ribbon or cord into a bow. Slip a bead on each end of a piece of **wide ribbon** about 30cm long and knot the ends.

3. Sew each feathery bow to the ribbon. Wear your choker to a special party.

3

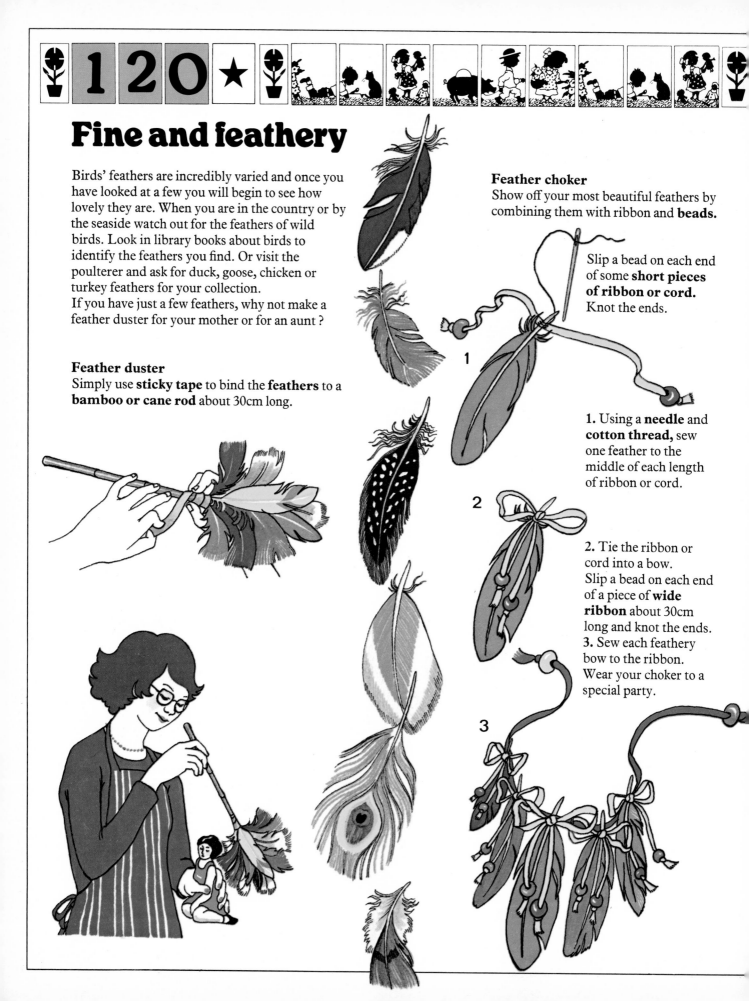

More mail please!

Stamp collecting is a popular hobby everywhere. Some stamps are collected because they are rare and valuable and others are saved up because of their attractive designs.

You could choose a subject, or a theme, for your own collection – what about stamps showing animals, or sports or famous paintings ?

The best way to look at the designs on stamps is through a magnifying glass.

Removing stamps

Never tear **stamps** from an envelope.

1. Use **scissors** to cut the stamp off, leaving 2cm of paper all round.

Fill a **shallow dish** with **cold water.**

2. Float your stamps in it, face upward, for about 15 minutes. Lift out the stamps with **tweezers.**

Peel off the paper. Put the stamps, face downward, on a sheet of **blotting paper.** Leave them to dry.

3. Press them between the pages of an **old book** overnight.

Zigzag folder

Most people put their stamps in an album. A folder is an interesting and different idea.

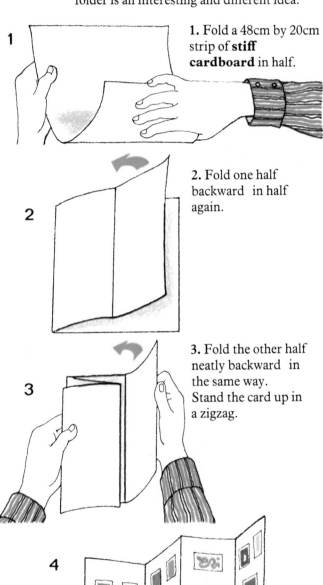

1. Fold a 48cm by 20cm strip of **stiff cardboard** in half.

2. Fold one half backward in half again.

3. Fold the other half neatly backward in the same way. Stand the card up in a zigzag.

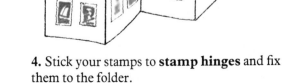

4. Stick your stamps to **stamp hinges** and fix them to the folder.

Odd one out

Think where you would find all these things, and then decide which is the odd one out in the group.
(The answer is given in the back of the book.)

Missing number

Which number should go in the blank square?

1	2	3	4	?	6

Five, because each number increases by one.
The puzzle below is similar, but a tiny bit harder.
Which number goes in the blank square?

2	3	5	?	12	17

(The answer is in the back of the book.)

Puzzling trio

Find **one coloured and two white scarves or handkerchiefs.** Knot them together so that two white ones are together and the coloured one is at the end.
Can you put the coloured scarf between the two white ones without untying any knots?
Here's a clue: one of the Magic projects in the previous pages showed a way of tying ribbons to perform a similar trick.
(The method is given in the back of the book.)

Tied in knots

To work this puzzle out, test it. You will need a friend to help you and two pieces of **string,** each about 80cm long.

Use one length of string to tie your friend's wrists together loosely. Loop the second length of string over the first length, and then loosely tie your own wrists together with the second length.

Can you and your friend work out how to untangle yourselves without breaking or untying the string? (The Answers in the back of the book show how it's done.)

Six buckets

Here is a row of six buckets. The first three buckets have water in them but the last three are empty.

By touching only one bucket, how can you make the row have alternate full and empty buckets? (There is a very simple solution and it is given in the back of the book.)

Lucky strike

Arrange **12 used matches** to make four equal squares as shown.

By moving only *three* matches, try to make three equal squares.

(The way to do it is shown in the back of the book.)

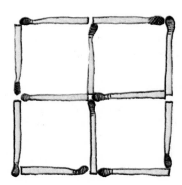

Jumping coin

Make a coin move without touching it.
Put a **small coin** on top of a **bottle** that has some **lemonade or other gassy drink** in it.
Hold the bottle tightly in both hands round the part that contains the drink.
The coin will begin to jump up and down.
The warmth of your hands makes the gas in the drink expand. As it tries to escape from the bottle, it pushes up the coin.

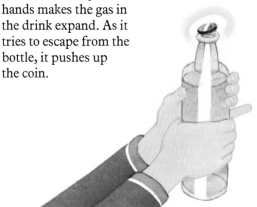

Mighty balloon

This specially-prepared balloon won't burst when you push a **pin** in at the right place.
Put a square of **transparent sticky tape** on an **inflated balloon**.

★★★★ Performance ★★★★

Tell your audience that you have an unburstable balloon. (They probably won't believe you.)
Push a pin into the balloon through the tape.
The balloon won't burst.

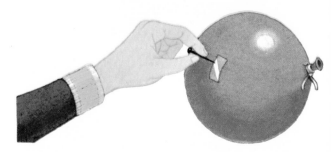

Salt and pepper

No secret preparation is needed for this trick.
Use a **pencil** to write 'Salt', 'Pepper', 'Salt' on a piece of **thin cardboard**. Tear the card in three and put the pieces in a **box.**
Tell your audience you can read the words without looking, then close your eyes and pick the card which says, 'Pepper'.
Picking the right card is easy. Because it is in the middle, the 'Pepper' card has two jagged edges when torn. All you have to do is feel the edges of the cards in the box.

Stick-up

This pencil seems to stick to your hand.
Show the spectators a **pencil** in your left hand, turning the back of your hand toward them.
Grasp your left wrist with your right hand.
The audience now sees the pencil stuck to it.

What no one sees is your right forefinger holding the pencil in your left palm.

Butterfly net

With this simple net you can catch butterflies, make drawings and identify them from library books. *Never kill butterflies.*

1. With **scissors,** cut the fine mesh from an **old plastic sieve** so that only the frame and handle are left.

1

2. With **string,** bind the handle to a **bamboo or cane rod** 50cm long.

2

3. Use a **tape measure** to measure the frame's circumference.

3

4. Cut a piece of **fine net** into a triangle. The top of the net should be the same measurement as the circumference of the frame.

4

25cm

5

Use a **needle** and **cotton thread** to join the sides of the net.
5. Attach it to the frame by sewing over the frame and through the top of the net.

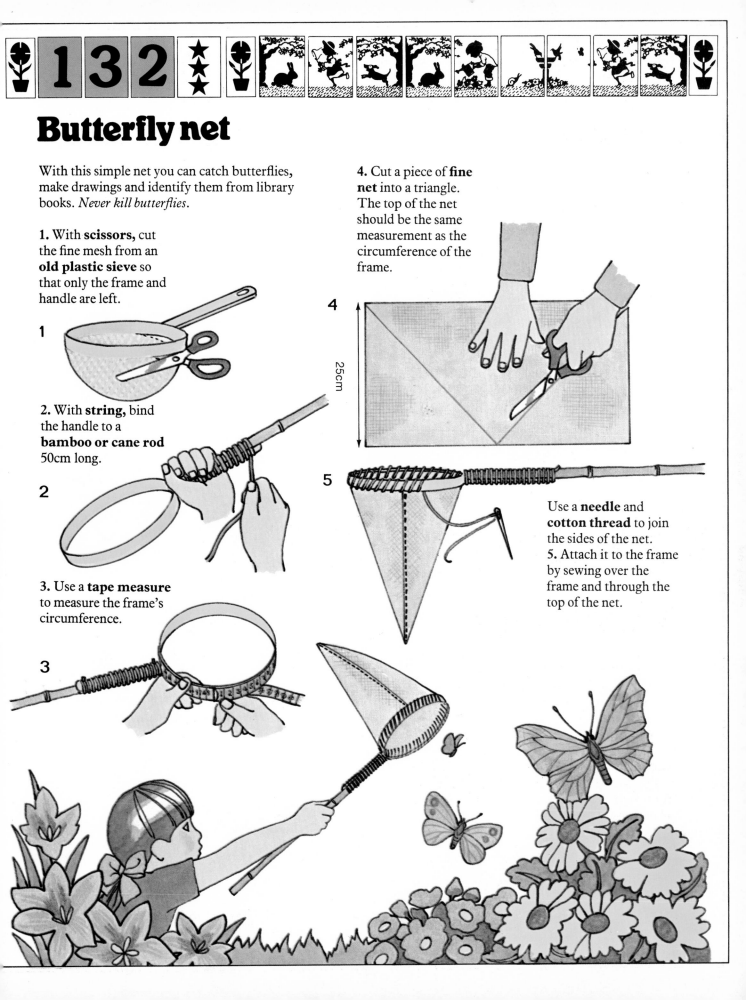

Butterfly farm

Caterpillars, as everyone knows, change into butterflies. If you prepare a special cage and find a caterpillar in the summer, you can watch this change yourself.

1. Ask an adult to punch some holes in the lid of a **shallow tin** with an **awl or a hammer and nail.** With **string** and a **ruler,** measure the tin's circumference.

2. Cut a piece of **clear, stiff plastic or acetate** (from an art shop) 50cm high and 2cm wider than the tin's circumference.

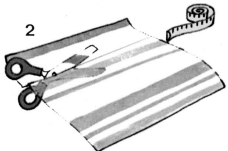

3. Use **strong glue** to join the edges of the plastic, overlapping them so that the plastic cylinder will just fit into the base of the tin.
Put the cylinder in the base of the tin.
Cut a **nylon stocking** to fit over the top.

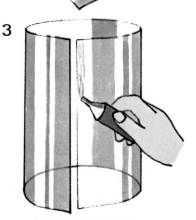

4. Carefully put the lid of the tin on the cylinder.

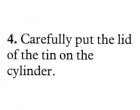

5. Put a layer of **soil** in the tin.

6. Put a **small jar of water** into the soil. Your cage is ready. Now look on grasses and plants or in hedges for a **caterpillar.** (A clue is chewed leaves.) Take some of the plant, too. This is the **caterpillar's food.**

7. Put the plant in the jar of water to keep it fresh and put your caterpillar on the plant. Put in fresh food when the caterpillar has eaten the leaves.
When the butterfly emerges, set it free.

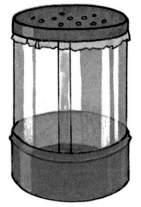

Pressed flowers

If you choose perfect flowers for pressing, you can make all kinds of beautiful things.
Here's how to press flowers and how to make a calendar.

1. Separate **flowers** from their stems.

Lay them face downward between **newspaper.**
2. Put **books** on top and leave the flowers for a few days.
Change the newspaper and leave them for another few days.

Calendar
Use **glue** to stick a **calendar** on the bottom half of a sheet of **coloured cardboard.**
1. Draw a design on the top in **pencil.**

2. Carefully glue some **pressed flowers** on your design.

Bouncing conkers

A well-known game is played with conkers, or horse-chestnuts. You can also make a bouncing mobile with them.
Collect some **conkers** in the autumn and varnish them with **polyurethane varnish** and a **brush** to help preserve their colour.
Ask an adult to pierce a hole right through the conkers with a **meat skewer.**
Knot one end of a piece of **thin elastic** and thread it through a conker.
Do the same with the other conkers.
Tie the lengths of elastic round a **bamboo or cane rod.** Use **string** to suspend the rod from a curtain rail and watch the conkers bounce.

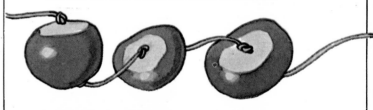

All eyes

Grow a potato into an attractive trailing plant.
Choose a **potato with lots of 'eyes'.**
Push **toothpicks** into the potato and rest it in a **jar of water** so that the bottom of the potato just touches the water.
Put the jar in a cool, dark place until the potato has sprouted both roots and shoots.
When it is ready, use a **knife** to cut off all but one or two of the potato shoots.
Put some **pebbles** in the bottom of a **flowerpot.**
Fill the pot with **damp potting soil.**
Then plant the potato in the pot. Don't forget to water it when the soil feels dry.

Spatter pictures

This can be messy, so be sure to wear an **apron** and remember to clear up afterwards.

1. Spread out a sheet of **newspaper** and lay a sheet of **white or coloured paper** on it.

2. Use **pins** to fix a **leaf or another flat object** to the paper.
Mix some **poster paint** with a little **water.**
Don't make it too thin.

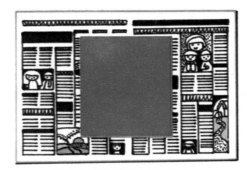

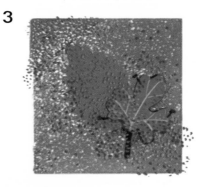

3. Pin a **second leaf or another flat object** to the paper, overlapping the first shape a little. Spatter it with a different colour.

If you use several colours, spatter each one *lightly* or your picture will soon get messy.

Dip an **old toothbrush** in the paint. Hold an **old comb** over the paper and rub the toothbrush too and fro across the teeth of the comb.

When the paper is spattered all over, wait three minutes and then lift off the leaf.

Cook a frame

This picture frame is only for looking at, not for eating! **Ask an adult** to help you cook it.

1. Use a **rolling-pin** to roll out the **dough** until it is 1cm thick.

Trim it to a square with a **kitchen knife** and keep the left-over scraps.

1

Centre a **picture** on the square.

2. With the knife, mark an outline a bit larger than the picture all round.

2

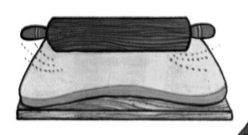

3

3. Press with your fingertips inside the outline to make a slight hollow.

Dough recipe

1 cup hot water
¾ cup salt
3 cups flour

Mix the salt and water in a **bowl.** Leave it to cool. Mix in the flour with your hands. Work fast – this dough soon goes brittle!

4. Roll and cut the dough scraps into little balls, thin sausages and other shapes.

Dab the back of the shapes with a little **water** and press them on to the dough frame.

4

Cook the frame until it is quite dry (30-40 minutes) in an **oven** set at 190°C (Mark 5).

5. Paint the frame with **acrylic paints** and use **glue** to stick the picture in the hollow.

5

Water cooler

See how to keep water cool in the sunshine.
You will need **two glass jars** and **two cotton tea-towels**.
1. Fill both glass jars with **water**.

Wrap a tea-towel round one glass jar.
2. Soak the other tea-towel in water and wrap it tightly round the other glass jar.
Put both jars outside in the sun. (Or put them in a warm linen cupboard.)

Feel the wet tea-towel about every half-hour.
3. When it is dry, take off both tea-towels and feel the jars with your hands.
The jar that was wrapped in the wet tea-towel will feel cooler than the other jar.

This is because the water in the wet tea-towel *evaporates* (or mixes with the dry air round the tea-towel). As it does this, it draws heat from the jar inside, so keeping the jar cool.
A similar thing happens when you perspire: as the sweat evaporates from your skin, it draws heat from your body and cools you down.

Soft potato

Ask a friend to try to push an ordinary **drinking straw** into a **raw potato.**
The straw will probably bend and the potato will remain exactly the same.
Now you can show how it's done.
Grip the straw firmly between your thumb and first finger a few centimetres from one end.
Quickly thrust the straw at the potato.
You should make a hole in the potato.
Your friend will be amazed, so explain why the straw pierces the potato.
When you grip and thrust quickly in this way, air is held inside the straw. This makes the sides of the straw stronger, which stops it bending as it hits the potato.

Draw an oval

Draw an oval using a **pair of compasses.**
Roll a piece of **stiff cardboard** about 30cm by 20cm into a cylinder.
Put **masking tape** on the join.
Roll a sheet of **paper** the same size round the cylinder and fix the join with masking tape.
Set a pair of compasses to a radius of about 8cm.
Push the point of the compasses into the paper and card.
Turn the **pencil** round.
Remove the compasses and unwrap the paper.
You have an oval!

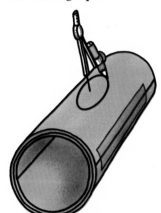

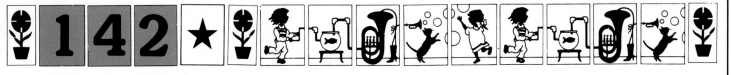
Spinning vision

This game is a lot of fun and shows you how your brain looks at pictures or images.

Use a **pencil** and a **pair of compasses** to draw a circle 15cm across on **stiff cardboard.**

1. Cut it out with **scissors.** Cut the scraps into several 1.5cm squares.
Cut a **paper** circle 1cm smaller.

2. Fold the paper circle in half.
Repeat this step four more times.
Open out the paper circle and lay it on the cardboard circle.

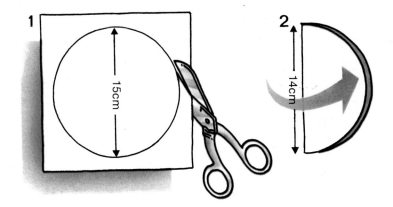

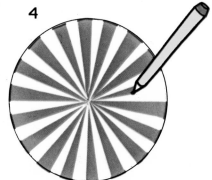

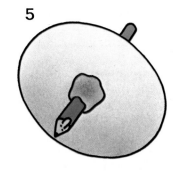

3. Use a **felt-tipped pen** to mark equal sections on the card, using the folds of the paper as a guide.
Join the marks across the circle.

4. Colour the alternate sections.
Make a hole in the cardboard circle with the point of the scissors.

Push a pencil through the hole.
5. Mould **plasticine** round the pencil and on to the card about 4cm from the sharpened end.

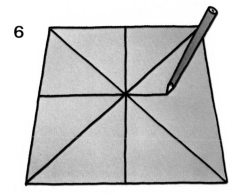

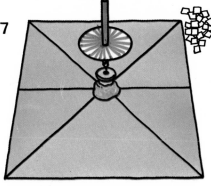

How to play
Spin the circle quickly.
Drop a **square of cardboard** on it.
It will fly off on to the board.
See if you can hit each segment.

When you spin the circle the white and coloured segments seem to mix together. That's because each time a picture reaches your brain it stays there for a fraction of a second.
This is called *persistence of vision.*

6. Divide a **big sheet of paper** (about 40cm square) into eight equal segments as shown.

Fix a **cotton reel** to the middle of the paper with plasticine.
7. Stand the pencil in it.

Forgotten planet

Your spaceship has crash-landed on a strange planet that is still covered with the men and monsters from prehistoric times.

You need to reach Mission Control Headquarters to radio for help, but first you encounter a number of hazards on the way.

All the players take it in turns to throw a **dice** and the first one to throw a six starts. Different-coloured **counters** are used by the players.

Starting at square one, move your counter according to the number you have thrown on the dice. Every time you land on a square which holds the bottom of a rocket, you can zoom to the top. Every time you meet the head of a monster, you must slide right down to the tip of its tail. You will also meet other helps and hazards on your journey.

The player who reaches Mission Control Headquarters (Square 100) first, wins the Forgotten Planet game.

Sliding coins

Arrange **six coins** in a pyramid as shown.
By *sliding* only four coins to different places, make
the pyramid into a circle.

Rule: when moving a coin into a new position,
it *must* touch two other coins.
(The method is shown in the back of the book.)

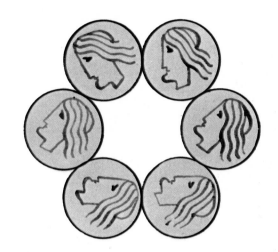

Take your pick

Can you name the fruits on this strange tree?
(The fruits are given in the Answers in the back of
the book.)

Eskimo family

Here is a puzzle set in Alaska where the Eskimo
people live in ice houses called *igloos*.
A little Eskimo and a big Eskimo are building a
new igloo together.
They cut the blocks of ice to size, and then
arrange them one on top of the other.
The little Eskimo is the big Eskimo's son.
But the big Eskimo is not the little Eskimo's
father.
Who is the big Eskimo? (That is, can you tell
what is the family relationship between the big
and the little Eskimo?)
(The answer is given in the back of the book.)

Hat trick

Each one of these characters is wearing the wrong hat. Can you dress them correctly?
(The answers are given in the back of the book.)

sailor   indian

cowboy   chinaman

clown   footballer

Birthday cake

How can you cut this cake into eight equal portions by making only three cuts?
A clue: four pieces would have no icing.
(The solution is given in the Answers at the back of the book.)

A dotty one

Can you join up all the dots by drawing only four straight lines? You must not take your **pencil** off the **paper** but you can draw beyond the frame of the dots if you want to.
(Look in the back of the book for the method.)

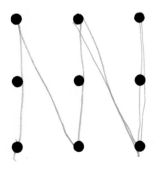

Family photographs

Collecting photographs can be an amusing hobby. Very old portrait photographs might make you laugh because the people look so stiff. They had to sit absolutely still for quite a few minutes while a photograph was taken.

You could make a collection of family photographs starting from recently-taken ones and going back to the oldest ones you can find. Ask your parents, grandparents or aunts and uncles for photographs. Look at the photographs closely to see how fashions and hairstyles have changed or how transport has developed. Don't forget to look for family resemblances – who do you think you look like in your family?

Frames

Most people keep their photographs in an album but you might like to make frames for the most interesting photographs in your collection.

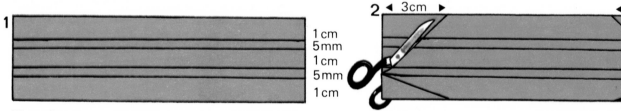

1

1 cm
5mm
1 cm
5mm
1 cm

Use **scissors** to cut two sheets of **paper** 18cm by 4cm and two sheets 16cm by 4cm.

2 ◄ 3cm ►   ◄ 3cm ►

1. With a **ruler** and **pencil,** mark four lines across each sheet of paper at intervals of 1cm, 5mm, 1cm, 5mm and 1cm as shown.

Mark 3cm down from all the top and bottom edges of the sheets.
2. Cut off these corners.

3. Fold each sheet along the lines and use **glue** to stick them down.

4

Cut a sheet of **white cardboard** 17cm by 13cm.
4. Glue the folded paper frame round the cardboard, then glue your **photograph** in the middle.

Seed jewelry

There are plenty of places to look for seeds if you want to collect them as a hobby. Look in the countryside, the garden or park after plants have flowered. In the autumn you can find seeds that have fallen from trees such as beech and oak. Or save the pips and seeds from fruit you have eaten. Once you have collected a variety of seeds, why not make some jewelry with them? Tiny melon, orange or apple seeds are pretty enough for a necklace or brooch.
Always wash and dry pips or seeds first.

Seed necklace
Thread a **needle** with a piece of **thin elastic** and tie a knot in one end.
Push the needle into **melon or apple seeds** and thread them on to the elastic.
When you have enough, remove the needle and tie the ends of the elastic together.

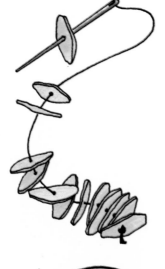

Seed brooch
Cut a piece of **stiff cardboard** to the shape you want.
1. Fix a **safety-pin** to the back of it with **sticky tape.**

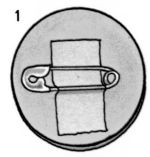

2. Arrange **small seeds** (apple, orange or melon) on the front. Use **glue** to stick each one into place. Let the glue dry.

Quick stickers

Stickers are a form of advertising. If you ask nicely and explain that you are collecting stickers, most firms will give you a few. Ask at travel agents, garages and shops. You'll see that stickers advertise almost everything!
Use them to decorate books, belts or an apron.

Sticker apron
Here's an idea for a very unusual apron. Make it for yourself or as a gift for someone else.

Use **scissors** to cut out the shape of the apron from **American cloth or plastic-coated cloth.** (You don't need to hem this kind.)
Cut two long pieces of **tape** to make apron ties and one short piece to go round the neck.
With a **needle** and **strong cotton thread,** sew the pieces of tape to the apron.
Now decorate the apron with **stickers.** You'll find that they stick very easily to plastic.

Silhouette portrait

A *silhouette* is an outline. Here is an easy way to make a silhouette portrait of your friend.

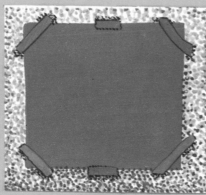

1. Ask a friend to sit sideways against a **wall.**

2. Fix a sheet of **paper** to the wall with **masking tape.**

3. Take the lampshade off a **table lamp.**

4. Make the room as dark as possible by closing doors and drawing curtains.

5. Switch on the lamp and move it close to your friend.

6. Outline the shadow with **pencil.** Cut it out with **scissors** and use **glue** to stick it to **cardboard.**

Glue a frame of **coloured paper** round the picture.

Scratch painting

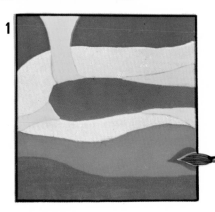

This is an amazing kind of painting because the colours actually appear from behind a thick surface of black wax crayon.

1. Using **poster or acrylic paints,** make big blocks of colour on a sheet of **thick paper.** Completely cover the paper with paint.

2. When the paint is quite dry, scribble all over the paper with **black wax crayon.**
Press down hard and completely cover the painted colours with crayon.

With a **nail or a knitting needle** (or any other sharp object) scratch a picture in the wax so that the colours appear.

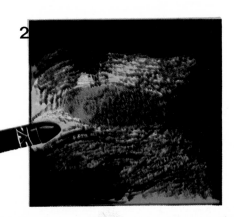

Pond study

If you are lucky enough to have a pond in your garden or near your home, you can discover the fascinating world that exists beneath the water.

Make a net by binding a **wire sieve** to a 1 metre-long **pole** with **strong string.** Or you can make a butterfly net as shown on Project 132. You will also need a **magnifying glass,** a **white dish** for viewing specimens and a **jar** for taking specimens home with you.

Ask an adult to come with you if the pond is deep, and approach it carefully. First watch the surface of the pond. You should be able to see tiny insects moving on the water. You may see the *larvae* (grubs) of other insects hanging below the surface of the water.

Now take your net and scoop it into the water round the edge of the pond. Then stretch out and scoop into the middle of the pond. (Be careful you don't lose your balance!) You might catch newts, tadpoles and beetles as well as tinier plants and animals in this way.

1. Put anything you catch into the dish and examine it with the magnifying glass. Then you could put the creatures back in the pond.

2. If you want to take a few newts or tadpoles home, prepare a jar for them. Put some **sand** in the bottom of the jar, plant some **pondweed** in it and fill the jar with **water.** Feed the newts with worms. Tadpoles eat meat which you can hang from the edge of the jar with string.

Dial-a-sun

Before clocks and watches were invented, everyone measured time by the sun. Make a sundial and do the same.

Press a lump of **plasticine** on to the middle of a sheet of **cardboard** about 30cm square.
1. Push the blunt end of a **pencil** into the plasticine at an angle.

1

Put the sundial outside in the sun.
Use a **clock or watch** to tell the time.
2. On the hour, make a mark at the point where the shadow of the pencil falls on the card.

2

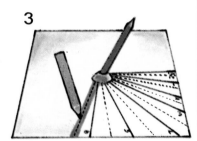

3. At every half-hour after that, write the time where the shadow falls.
Do this from early morning till sunset.

3

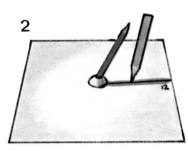

4. Once you have marked your sundial, you can tell the time without a watch as long as the sun is shining. Always leave the sundial facing the same way. If you like, decorate the clock face and varnish the whole sundial.

4

Sweeping start

This is the sort of broom that witches were supposed to have flown on. You can use it to sweep up leaves, even if you can't fly!

1

Find a good **straight branch** 1.5 metres long.
1. Strip off any side branches.

2. Bind some **strong string** to the branch about 20cm from one end.

2

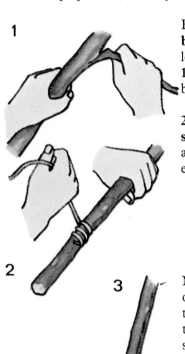

3

Now tie the first layer of **long, sweepy twigs** to the branch, binding them tightly with more string.
Keep adding layers of twigs until your broom is thick.

3. Bind the outside layer very tightly, using lots of string.
You need to make a band of string at least 5cm or 6cm wide.

Flick book

This book changes from an empty book to a full stamp album and back again before your eyes! With **scissors** cut a narrow strip from the edge of every other page in an **old exercise book**.
1. On every double page where the short page falls on the right-hand side, stick some **stamps**.

1

2. Where the short page falls on the left, leave the pages completely blank.

2

★ ★ ★ ★ Performance ★ ★ ★ ★

3. Hold the book in front of you and flick through the pages with your left hand. The book appears to be full of stamps.
4. Turn the book over and flick the pages the other way, with your right hand. The book now appears to be empty.

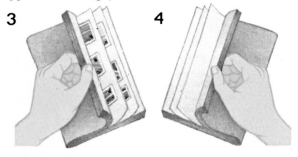

Mathemagic

Your audience will have to do some work, too, when you perform this trick.

★ ★ ★ ★ Performance ★ ★ ★ ★

1

Hand a friend a sheet of **paper** and a **pencil**.
1. Ask your friend to draw a square and write in it any number from one to nine, without letting you see it.

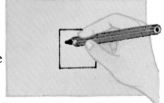

2. Tell your friend to write the same number to the right and the left of the square.

2
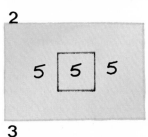

3. Now ask him to write the figure 3 above and below the square.

3
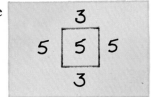

Now your friend should add up all the numbers on the sheet of paper and tell you the total. As soon as you know the total, you can tell your friend the number he or she originally wrote in the square.

How you do it
Divide your friend's total by three.
Take away two and the answer is the number in the square.
In the example shown in the pictures, your friend will tell you that the total is 21 (5+5+5+3+3). When you divide by three you get seven (21÷3); then seven minus two equals five (7−2=5).

All change

Find the two, three, four and five of hearts and of spades in an **old pack of cards.**

1. Use **scissors** to cut the two, three and four of hearts in half from corner to corner.

1

2. Use **glue** to stick one half of each card to the face of the two, three and four of spades.

2

3. Arrange the three special cards in a fan shape. Place a five of hearts on top so it looks as if you are holding the two, three, four and five of hearts. Hide the five of spades at the back of the fan.

3

 ★ ★ ★ ★ **Performance** ★ ★ ★ ★

Show the red cards to your audience, then close the cards into a small pack.
Turn the cards over.
Put the five of hearts to the back of the pack.
Bring the five of spades to the front.
Turn the pack upside-down.
Open out the cards, making sure you keep the five of hearts hidden. It will look as if they have changed from red to black.

Ring vanish

Keep this trick up your sleeve for moments when you and your friends are feeling bored!
Tie a piece of **elastic** to a **ring.** The elastic should be about three-quarters the length of your arm.

1. Tie the other end of the elastic to a **safety-pin.**

1

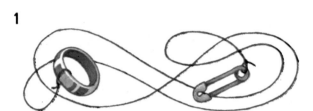

Fasten the pin inside the top of the right sleeve of your jumper.

2. Put the ring on one of your right fingers and then put your jumper on.

2

★ ★ ★ ★ **Performance** ★ ★ ★ ★

3. Take the ring off your finger with the left hand. Be careful not to show the elastic.
Hold the ring between your right forefinger and thumb. Pretend to throw the ring into the air.
As you let go it disappears (up your sleeve)!

3

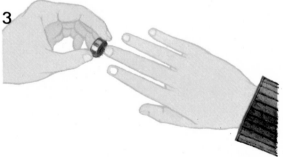

Marble bridges

Here is a new way of playing marbles, but you need to make a bridge before you start playing. To make the bridge, find an old **shoe box.** With a **pencil,** draw four arches along one side. Then cut out the arches with **scissors,** and write a number above each one.

To play the game, each player should have an equal number of **marbles.** One player is the 'bridge keeper' but he does not shoot. With a **piece of string or a ruler,** make a starting line about two metres away from the bridge. Each player in turn tries to shoot a marble into one of the arches. For each marble which goes through, he receives from the 'bridge keeper' the number of marbles corresponding to the number above the arch. He also receives his 'shooter' back. If the 'shooter' does not go through the arch, it belongs to the 'bridge keeper'. The game ends when each player has had ten shots. The player with the most marbles is the winner.

What's missing?

Any number of people can play this game, but they all need a sharp eye and a good memory. Find as many **household objects** as you can – packets, tins, soap, spoons and so on.

Put them all on a table – but don't forget to **ask an adult** before you raid the cupboards. Give every player a piece of **paper** and a **pencil.** Pick someone to be an observer. The players have a good look at the objects on the table. Then they all leave the room except one player and the observer. The player who is left removes one object from the table. The observer writes down the name of the object and puts it out of sight. The other players return and write down what is missing from the table. All the players take it in turns to remove an object. Then they compare their lists with the observer's list. The one with the most correct missing objects is the winner.

Twenty questions

Thinking hard can be fun. Choose your
questions carefully to win this game.
One player thinks of an object, but mustn't say
what it is. The only thing he tells other players
is whether it is 'animal', 'vegetable' or 'mineral'.
For example, a whale and a fly are both 'animal'.
An onion is 'vegetable' but so is a book because
paper is made from trees. A tin of baked beans is
'vegetable' (beans) and 'mineral' (tin).
The other players can now ask twenty questions
to try to find out what the object is. The person
who thought of the object must only answer 'Yes'
or 'No'.
If the other players guess the object before twenty
questions are up, someone else thinks of an object
and the game starts again.

Hunt the beast

This is a good game for a party or for two friends.
Two players are chosen as the 'hunter' and
'beast'. Tie a **blindfold** round the 'hunter's' eyes
and give him a **rolled-up newspaper.**
The 'hunter' calls out 'Where are you beast?' and
the other player must roar like a wild animal and
try to escape.
The 'hunter' has to guess where the 'beast' is and
try to whack him with the newspaper. If he
succeeds in catching the 'beast' the players
change places.
This game is best played out of doors, but if there
are a lot of people indoors, they can form a circle
to stop people bumping into the furniture.

Donkey's tail

This is a hilarious game for a party.
Find or draw a **large picture of a donkey** (or
any other animal with a tail). Cut off the tail and
stick a drawing-pin through the top.
Then fix the picture to the wall with **drawing-
pins or masking tape** at about eye level.
Make a blindfold with an **old scarf.** Each player
in turn should be blindfolded and the tail put in
his hand. He must try to pin the tail as nearly as
possible to the right place on the donkey. The
other players can join in the game by giving
directions, for example – 'Move to the right!',
'Further down!', 'You're getting warmer!'.
To make the game harder, the blindfolded player
can be spun round a couple of times.

Potato people

You can make a potato family or even a royal family with some scraps from around the house.
Collect together a
large, medium and a
small potato.

Using **pins** and **glue**, attach **buttons** for eyes, scraps of **cloth** for clothes and **wool** for hair.
With **sequins, gold braid** and scraps of **velvet,** make the King and his Royal Potato Family.

Sound sense

The shape of this cone concentrates sound. You can use it as a microphone and talk to people who are far away; or use it as an amplifier and listen through it to sounds coming from far away or very quiet sounds.

1. Bend a **large piece of cardboard** about 50cm by 40cm to make a cone shape. Fix it with **sticky tape.**

1

2. Bend a **smaller piece of cardboard** about 40cm by 25cm round to cover the gap in the cone. Stick it in place on the cone. Cut the corners with **scissors** to make the two ends of the cone into neat circles.

2

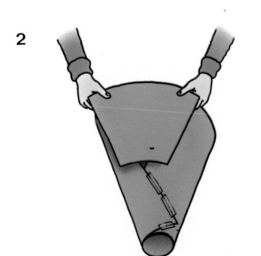

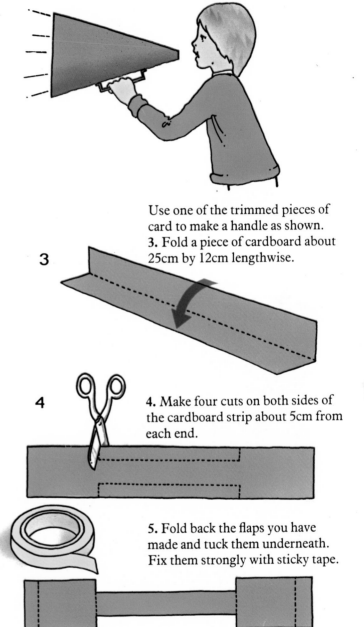

Use one of the trimmed pieces of card to make a handle as shown.

3. Fold a piece of cardboard about 25cm by 12cm lengthwise.

3

4

4. Make four cuts on both sides of the cardboard strip about 5cm from each end.

5. Fold back the flaps you have made and tuck them underneath. Fix them strongly with sticky tape.

5

6. Bend the handle as shown and join it to the cone.

6

20.

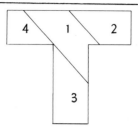

21. He takes the hen across to the bank. He returns alone. He then rows the fox across, leaves it, and brings back the hen. Then he takes the grain across, leaves it with the fox, and returns finally for the hen.

22.

42. Erect the post so the sign with the name of the village you have come from points down that road. Then the signs will be right.

43.

Start at 'A' or 'B' and follow the unbroken lines.

44. The pairs are: 1+9, 2+8, 4+12, 5+14, 7+13, 10+16. There are four odd cars left.

45. Rhinoceros, donkey, tiger, shark, tortoise, kangaroo.

46. The triangles are: ABC, ABD, ABE, ABF, ABG, ABH, ACD, ACE, ACI, ADE, ADH, AEF, AEG, AEI, AFG, BCD, BCE, BCG, BCH, BCJ, BDE, BDF, BEJ, BGH, CDE, CDH, CDI, CDJ, CEG, CHJ, DEF, DEI, DEJ, DIJ, EFI.

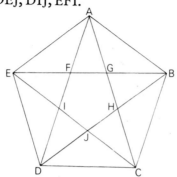

70.

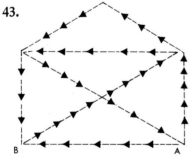

71.

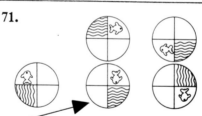

This fish is the odd one out because it is swimming in an anti-clockwise direction from the sea, instead of clockwise.

72.

103. a,g,f,c,h,b,e,d.

104. Eleven.

105. He lets air out of each tyre until the lorry sinks by 2.5cm.

106.

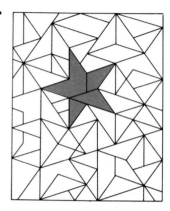

122. The star, because all the others are household objects.

123. Eight, because the numbers increase by +1, +2, +3, +4, +5.

124. Knot all three together so that they form a circle.

125.

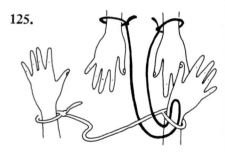

Push your friend's string *under* the loop on your wrist. Make the loop big enough so that you can slip it over your hand.

126. Empty the second bucket into the fifth, and then return it to its original position.

127.

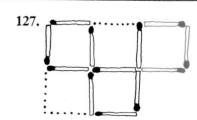

144.

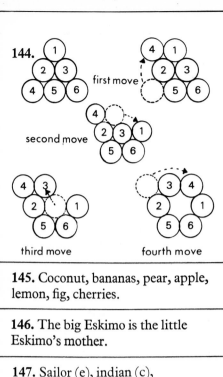

145. Coconut, bananas, pear, apple, lemon, fig, cherries.

146. The big Eskimo is the little Eskimo's mother.

147. Sailor (e), indian (c), cowboy (f), chinaman (b), clown (a), footballer (d).

148.

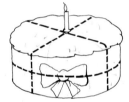

149.